SHENANDOAH UNIVERSITY LIBRARY
WINCHESTER, VA 22601

Jordan L. Harding

COLLECTION

Class of
1950

Doctor of Laws (Honorary)
2002

SHENANDOAH
UNIVERSITY

SHENANDOAH UNIVERSITY LIBRARY
WINCHESTER, VA 22601

PROPHETIC VOICES IN CONTEMPORARY THEOLOGY

SHENANDOAH UNIVERSITY LIBRARY
WINCHESTER, VA 22601

ALVIN C. PORTEOUS

PROPHETIC VOICES IN CONTEMPORARY THEOLOGY

The Theological Renaissance and the Renewal of the Church

ABINGDON PRESS
NASHVILLE • NEW YORK

4-3-07

PROPHETIC VOICES IN
CONTEMPORARY THEOLOGY

Copyright © 1966 by Abingdon Press

All rights in this book are reserved.
No part of the book may be reproduced in any manner whatsoever without written permission of the publishers except brief quotations embodied in critical articles or reviews. For information address Abingdon Press, Nashville, Tennessee.

ISBN 0-687-34410-7
Library of Congress Catalog Card Number: 66-15000

Quotations from *Prisoner for God* by Dietrich Bonhoeffer are reprinted with permission of The Macmillan Company and SCM Ltd. Copyright 1953, The Macmillan Company.
Quotations from *Ethics* by Dietrich Bonhoeffer are reprinted with permission of The Macmillan Company and SCM Ltd. Copyright 1955, The Macmillan Company.

BT
28
.P67
P7
1966

SET UP, PRINTED, AND BOUND BY THE PARTHENON PRESS, AT NASHVILLE, TENNESSEE, UNITED STATES OF AMERICA

To My Wife
Marion

PREFACE

Voices calling for the renewal of the church are being heard today in a rising crescendo. This is a book about some of the germinal insights of contemporary theologians which, in my judgment, are capable of shaping significantly the patterns of renewal in our time. It is written in the hope that it may make a modest contribution toward giving wider currency to some of the potentially explosive ideas which the theological renaissance of the last generation or so has bequeathed to the church. It has emerged as the product of a growing conviction that present currents of renewal can come to full tide only when the church is attuned to hear the prophetic voices of its own theologians and assimilate the results of their creative work into the mainstream of its life.

It has not been my purpose to provide a definitive summary of all important aspects of each theologian's thought. Comprehensive and critical analyses are readily available elsewhere. I have endeavored, rather, to expound and interpret those insights from their theologies which seem to hold the greatest promise for stimulating and informing the movement of renewal at work in the church today. I have not been unmindful of the dangers inherent in any such undertaking of violating the integrity of a man's thought by oversimplification, interpretation out of context, and the muting of critical analysis of important technical issues in the interests of brevity and effective communication. I have persevered in the effort, however, in the belief that, whatever nuances might be lost in the translation, it is imperative for the health of the church that the liberating and disturbing insights of these men be made accessible to a wider readership among both ministers and laymen.

I owe a debt of gratitude to a variety of individuals and groups whose suggestions and encouragement have contributed significantly to the final product: Dean Robert G. Torbet of Central Baptist Theological Seminary, without whose constant encouragement and friendly advice this project would not have come to fruition; President John C. Bennett and Professor Daniel Day Williams of Union Theological Seminary, under whose tutelage much of my interest in contemporary theology was originally kindled; Professors Reinhold Niebuhr and Paul Tillich, two of the principals of this study, in whose classes at Union I saw how readily a professorial robe can be transformed into a prophet's mantle; the Rev. R. C. Plant, minister of the Community Church in Canada's atomic energy research center at Deep River, Ontario, in whose parish, during two enjoyable summers, I learned much about the problems and possibilities of theological communication in a scientific age; ministers and laymen at theological conferences and continuing education institutes at the American Baptist Assembly at Green Lake, Wisconsin, and Roanridge, Missouri, whose reactions to some of the materials in the book provided helpful guidance; and, finally, my students and colleagues at Central Baptist Theological Seminary and Linfield College, who have furnished the indispensable stimulus and challenge for continuing creative work.

ALVIN C. PORTEOUS

CONTENTS

I

THE CHURCH AND ITS THEOLOGIANS

This book is written out of the conviction that a fateful gap has for too long existed between the church and its theologians. Some such hiatus between the world of the professional theologian and the ongoing life and work of the church is, of course, no novelty in Christian history. To some extent the theologian has always tended to occupy a world apart. Up to a point this emancipation from the pressures and harassments of institutional involvements can be justified as a necessary condition for the creative fulfillment of his calling. His very usefulness to the church in his capacity as a theologian can be said to require a measure of independence from the nagging immediacy of practical churchly concerns. Moreover, without such independence the theologian is unable to maintain a sufficiently transcendent perspective with respect to the church to be helpful to it in the articulation and criticism of its message.

Theologians in Exile

But freedom for the sake of responsible service and banishment into virtual exile are two quite different things! In many sections of the church today, the latter fate would seem more nearly to conform to the facts about the church's relationship to its theologians. One of the unfortunate developments of recent American church history, which has contributed to the rather unflattering "new shape of American religion" described by Martin Marty, has been the effectiveness with which the church has quarantined its theologians from the mainstream of its life. The result has been the disturbing paradox of a theologically inarticulate church content to eke out its existence on a meager diet of theological pabulum surrounded by a veritable galaxy of brilliant and prophetic theological minds.

The theological renaissance, which has been going on for several decades now, has so far apparently failed to "take" in large areas of American church life. The occasional preacher who reads his Barth and his Niebuhr and the even more rare "thoughtful layman" who tangles now and again at first or second hand with the theological greats of our time are the magnificent exceptions rather than the rule.

But even more important than the reading habits of the clergy or the laity is the failure of so much of the preaching and teaching of the church to reflect the constructive results of the theological labors of our generation. By and large the laymen of our churches have been barred from even a superficial acquaintance with the profound insights spawned by the theological dialogue which has been going on in recent years. For one reason or another, the ministry has failed to communicate to the laity any sense of the ferment which has been permeating the theological world with creative new ideas for several decades now. So radically is the church insulated from the work of the theologian that it comes to a layman as a great surprise, and to some as a profound relief, that certain traditional ideas concerning the inspiration of the Bible or the nature of Christ are no longer considered by leading theologians as valid expressions of Christian faith and thought. Their sense of emancipation is sometimes mingled with a feeling of betrayal that these liberating insights have been withheld from them so long.

Why is it that the church has thus pushed the work of the theologian into the backwaters and side-eddies rather than allow it to course freely through the main channels of its life? A variety of reasons might be cited. In some cases, no doubt, it is a matter of suspicion and hostility born of fear. In other sections of the church the problem may be more a question of indifference to what the theologian is doing than fear of its consequences in subverting cherished beliefs. Both attitudes, however, are symptomatic of a widely pervasive mood of anti-intellectualism which infects much of American culture today.[1] The attitude of hostility represents what might be called a "hard anti-intellectualism"; the attitude of indifference, a "soft anti-intellectualism."

Anti-intellectualism of the hard variety involves a positive resentment against the "eggheads" of our society. Some people who are willing to tolerate eggheads in other professions such as science, particularly when they come to realize that the prestige and power of their country may be dependent upon them, react with visceral intensity against the idea of eggheads in religion. The notion that

[1] Cf. Richard Hofstadter, *Anti-Intellectualism in American Life* (New York: Alfred A. Knopf, 1963) for a full-dress historical analysis of the roots of anti-intellectualism in the development of the religious, political, business, and educational life of America.

in matters religious they should ever have to defer to the judgments of an expert is anathema to them. No doubt this particular brand of anti-intellectualism is frequently rooted in a perverse interpretation of the doctrine of the priesthood of all believers. The Lutheran conviction that "every man must do his own believing as every man must do his own dying" is translated to mean that every man's ideas on theological matters are as good as any other man's; hence, there is no need of experts in theology. The sorry conclusion of such a line of reasoning is that theological truth becomes a matter of counting noses, and theological orthodoxy is made contingent upon the majority vote of a mass meeting at a church convention.

If this kind of hard anti-intellectualism is characteristic of the more conservative and theologically defensive wing of the church, it is the soft variety of the same disease which is likely to plague the more liberal and theologically tolerant branches of the church. Here the theologian is not regarded so much as a threat as an irrelevancy. Here you find yourself in a bland kind of nonintellectual milieu in which the hard theological questions are never raised. Whether this is the fault of the minister or the layman is difficult to say. In too many cases it would seem that the minister has never even tried to awaken his people from their theological slumbers or prod them into self-conscious theological reflection. In other cases he has long since given up such attempts, discouraged by the intellectual laziness and inertia of a people mesmerized by the comforts and securities of a materialistic, success-oriented culture.

While these two brands of anti-intellectualism may represent the forms in which the disease infects the conservative and liberal types of church, it is not uncommon for both of them to take refuge under one roof. Within the same congregation one can identify those who are almost pathologically suspicious of the theologian and those who couldn't care less whether he existed or not!

But hard or soft, anti-intellectualism, with its attendant de-emphasis on theology and disdain for what the theologian stands for, is a grave and cancerous growth in the life of the contemporary church. Its disturbing implications have been spelled out for us by Peter Berger in his provocative *The Noise of Solemn Assemblies.* "Theology," he writes, "provides criteria by which Christian churches can judge themselves. If these criteria are lost, the Christian faith becomes the night in which all cats are gray." "In the absence of theological criteria," Berger warns, "two very dangerous criteria will tend to take over—in the institutional area, the criterion of expediency; and in the personal area, that of experience." [2]

When a church or denomination ceases to be related to its theologians in a continuing creative tension, the basic decisions affecting its life are no longer informed by vital theological norms. The important question is, then, not "What is the mandate for the church in the light of a mature theological understanding of the nature of the gospel?" but "What does it take to maintain the institution of the church as a successful, going, and growing concern?" When the second question assumes the center of the stage, the minister finds himself more and more cast in the role of the caretaker of an institution rather than the prophet of God or the shepherd of souls. Increasingly, he becomes the victim of statistical standards of evaluation and in-

[2] (New York: Doubleday and Company, 1961), pp. 124-25.

stitutionally oriented conceptions of what constitutes success in his calling. He finds himself adopting goals and methods which can be much more readily justified on the grounds of their pragmatic usefulness in promoting a successful organization than for reasons of theological integrity. Thus, practical expediency displaces theological reflection and affirmation as the ultimate touchstone of the church's life.

On the personal level, as Berger has reminded us, the demise of theology leads to "the cult of experience." Both the pietism of the revivalist movements and theological liberalism have contributed to this tendency in much American Christianity to major on subjective religious experience at the expense of disciplined theological thinking. The result has been an inordinate emphasis on the importance of the right kind of religious feeling, accompanied by a fundamental disinterest in the question of truth. Thus in many churches a high premium is placed on a preacher's ability to generate the appropriate complex of feeling tones by the skillful use of pious phrases, doctrinal jargon, and well-worn ritual whose very familiarity guarantees a conditioned response. When truth is in this way subordinated to sentiment we have come to the stage when, as Berger puts it, "emotional pragmatism now takes the place of the honest confrontation with the Christian message." [3]

How the Theologian Serves the Church

These disquieting effects of the split between the church and its theologians underscore the need for a rediscovery

[3] *Ibid.,* p. 126.

by the church of the proper role of the theologian in relation to its life and witness. The way out of the theologian's Babylonian Captivity leads through a renewed awareness of how the theologian is capable of serving the church in positive and constructive ways which are essential to its health and integrity as the body of Christ in the world. The church is bound to languish spiritually as long as those who are charged with the theological task are compelled or allowed to do their work on the periphery of the church's life. When this is permitted to happen, theology becomes too much an esoteric enterprise, smelling too strongly of the academician's lamp, lacking vital connections with the living, throbbing concerns of the church as a community of faith and witness.

There is a brand of avant-garde theologian of recent vintage who maintains that intellectual and spiritual integrity require him to do his work quite apart from the church. Alienated from the traditional forms of the church's expression of its faith, and unable to affirm it in its present form as a vehicle of God's redemptive action, they opt for "a theology of waiting" or "a theology of silence." Thomas J. J. Altizer speaks for this kind of "secular theologian" when he writes that "contemporary theology must be alienated from the Church . . . and the theologian must exist outside the Church, he can neither proclaim the Word, celebrate the sacraments, nor rejoice in the presence of the Holy Spirit: before contemporary theology can become itself, it must first exist in silence.[4] Another younger theologian, William Hamilton, can no longer avoid saying No openly to the church, and insists

[4] Quoted by William Hamilton, "Thursday's Child: The Theologian Today and Tomorrow" in *Theology Today,* January, 1964, p. 490.

that the theologian of today "no longer has the energy or interest to answer ecclesiastical questions about 'What the Church Must Do to Revitalize Itself.' "[5]

As disturbing as this radical No to the church by some of the younger generation of theologians may be as a measure of their tragic estrangement from one another, it can hardly be said to represent the typical stance of the more influential theologians of our time. As we shall have occasion to observe throughout this book, those theologians who speak most powerfully and prophetically to the church today are men who have lived close enough to the church to sense the pulsebeat of its life and share the burden of its mission. They are men not only of intellectual genius but spiritual passion. Their passion is for a church renewed by the truth of the gospel and re-formed by a more authentic obedience to the commission of its Lord. Deeply involved in the life of the church as her loyal but not uncritical servants, they cast upon her "the same affectionate but sharp glance" which J. B. Priestly once said every loving wife gives to her husband.

Before proceeding to our examination of the thought of these men and its potential for the renewal of the church, we shall address ourselves briefly to the more general question, "How does the theologian serve the church?" We shall deal with this question, first of all, in the light of an understanding of the theologian's perennial task, and then in the context of the crisis in which Christendom, and more particularly the church in America, finds itself today.

How are we to understand the task of the theologian as a service to the church? Unquestionably the credit belongs

[5] *Ibid.*

to Karl Barth, more than to any other theologian in modern times, for recalling theology to its servant role within the church. He has taught us anew, what was a central conviction of the Reformers, that the only proper context for the doing of theology is the church. So determinative is this conviction for Barth that he has dramatized it by changing the title of his *magnum opus* from *Christian Dogmatics* to *Church Dogmatics*. This is to suggest that an authentically Christian theology is always a *church* theology, that is, a theology of and for the church. It is a constructive and systematic exposition of the faith by which the church lives which provides the church with the critical tools for judging the authenticity of its life and witness. In Barth's words, it is "the scientific test to which the Christian Church puts herself regarding the language about God which is peculiar to her." [6]

Such a conception of the theological task is rigorously functional rather than speculative. The theologian who is content to assume "the form of the servant" within the church has the best insurance against gnosticising tendencies in his work. He sees that his job is not to indulge his speculative urge to spin his own theories about ultimate reality; it is to give himself responsibly to the expository and critical task of testing the church's proclamation—both its preaching and its living—in a quite definite setting which is already defined for him, and with refer-

[6] Karl Barth, *Church Dogmatics* (Edinburgh: T. & T. Clark, 1936-60), I/1. Hereafter Barth's *Church Dogmatics* will be referred to as CD. It is interesting to note that Paul Tillich, whose theological method is at fundamental points at variance with Barth's is in full agreement that theology is a function of the church. "Theology, as a function of the Christian church, must serve the needs of the church." *Systematic Theology* (Chicago: University of Chicago Press, 1951), I, 3.

ence to a very particular norm to which he is bound in all his theological work. He sees it as his function in the church to keep the concrete realities of the church's life in constant tension with the revelatory action of God in Jesus Christ. His is the task of applying the test of the Word of God, as witnessed to in Scripture and as illuminated by the continuing theological conversations of the centuries, to the content of the church's preaching and the forms of its witness and service to the world.

Theology, then, is the church's means of questioning the authenticity of its own speech about God. It is a necessary and continuing function in the life of the church because of the fallibility of all preaching and teaching. Without the built-in corrective of a mature theology, which is itself constantly subjecting itself to critical revision, the preachers and teachers of the church can readily stray from fidelity to the Word of God in their expression of the Christian faith. In this perspective, theology is at once the intellectual expression of the church's repentance and the permanent possibility of the church's reform. This is not to say, of course, that the theologian can prescribe the content of sermons and teaching materials and practical programs. It is his more modest task to provide the conceptual tools by means of which these and other forms of the church's proclamation may be tested against the norm of God's self-revelation in Jesus Christ.

So far our description of the theologian's function in the church has followed lines which would meet with Barth's approval. There is a further dimension of the theologian's task, however, which I consider an essential part of his job description, which Barth would consider illegitimate. I would maintain that the theologian serves the church by testing its proclamation not only in terms of its faithfulness to the Word of God, but also in terms of its relevance to the contemporary human situation. In insisting on this latter kind of testing we are choosing as our mentors men like Paul Tillich and Rudolf Bultmann, who take seriously the apologetic task of theology as well as its kerygmatic function.[7]

The church needs help from its theologians not only in the systematic explication of its faith as this is found in the biblical witness. It also needs help in the formulation of this faith in terms which speak meaningfully and relevantly to modern man. It needs, to be sure, guardians against heresy; men who are commissioned to define and defend the boundaries of the citadel of Christian belief; men whose primary concern it is to protect the biblical integrity of the church's message against the erosion of alien ideologies. In performing this function with such prophetic vigor and scholarly thoroughness, Barth has left the church of our day immeasurably in his debt. But the church should expect more of its theologians than the clarification for itself of its own faith and the continual redigging of the wells from which that faith has flowed. It should expect from them also assistance in mediating that faith to unbelievers. This puts the theologian in the business of building bridges to unbelief. It requires of him a service to the church in terms of the needs not only of

[7] The term "apologetic," in this connection, refers to the attempt to exhibit the reasonableness and contemporary relevance of basic theological affirmations, i.e. to show the way in which they constitute viable answers to questions posed by our present historical situation. The term "kerygmatic" refers to theology's central task of explicating the meaning of the New Testament kerygma, which was the content of the early church's proclamation.

the "insider" but of the "outsider" as well. And since, as James E. Sellers has reminded us in a recent study of Christian communication,[8] the outsider is to be found inside the church as often as outside it, the apologetic or bridge-building function of the theologian becomes an especially urgent service to contemporary Christian preaching.

One might wish that we could dispose of the problem of communication to the outsider as easily as Barth by simply refusing to regard it as a legitimate concern of the Christian theologian. But is the matter really settled by affirming, as Barth does, that there are no real outsiders to the grace of God? [9] Is it really true, as he insists, that "the best way of dealing with 'unbelievers' . . . is . . . to treat them quietly, simply (remembering that Christ has died and risen also for them), as if their rejection of 'Christianity' was not to be taken seriously"? [10] Surely it may be questioned whether belief in the sovereignty and freedom of God's grace commits us to what would seem to be an unpardonable irresponsibility in Christian communication.

At any rate, most of the theologians who are subjects of this study *do* take modern man's rejection of Christianity seriously. They recognize, moreover, that much of this rejection may very well be a product of the church's failure in communication rather than the perversity of those who, in increasing numbers, are turning a deaf ear to its message. Accordingly, they see the need not only of preserving the basic affirmations and intentions of the biblical revela-

[8] *The Outsider and the Word of God* (Nashville: Abingdon Press, 1961), ch. 1.

[9] Karl Barth, *The Humanity of God* (Richmond: John Knox Press, 1960), pp. 58-59.

[10] John Baillie (ed.), *Natural Theology* (London: Centenary Press, 1946), p. 31.

tion, but also of formulating those affirmations and intentions in such a way that their meaning for man's concrete situation in today's world is clearly exhibited. Thus, Tillich has sought to correlate the Christian answers with the real questions which modern men are asking out of their situation of meaninglessness and despair. Bultmann has tried to remove what he considers to be a false stumbling block in the way of faith by means of his program of demythologizing the Bible. Bonhoeffer has searched for new forms of Christian witness to meet the challenge of "a world come of age." And Niebuhr has endeavored to show the relevance of a Christian view of man for the political and social dilemmas of our modern world. In an illuminating epigram Roger Hazelton has described the ideal balance between biblical integrity and contemporary relevance for which these men have striven. "Theological language," he writes, "needs spaciousness as well as specificity; it should be humanly relevant no less than Christianly recognizable." [11]

A Church in Crisis

Kerygmatic adequacy and apologetic effectiveness; these are the two fundamental criteria which the theologian uses in testing the church's understanding of its message and mission. Evidences are mounting that the church in America today is in the throes of a double-pronged crisis resulting from a failure to measure up to both these tests. On the one hand, it is in danger of surrendering its distinctively Christian substance to the encroachments of a

[11] Roger Hazelton, *New Accents in Contemporary Theology* (New York: Harper & Row, 1960), p. 50.

vague religiosity which shows signs of becoming the unofficial established religion of the nation. On the other, it is faced with a breakdown of communication with what is more and more frequently being referred to as a post-Christian culture, in which the traditional Christian symbols and theological formulations have been evacuated of meaning for large numbers of people.

It may, on the surface, seem unduly paradoxical to speak in the same breath of a revival of religious interest and a post-Christian era as both characterizing the current religious situation in America. But the paradox becomes more believable when the pseudo-Christian nature of the religious revival is brought to light, as it has been, almost to the point of tedium, in a number of sociological and theological critiques published in the last few years.[12]

A statement by Reinhold Niebuhr in 1955 is typical of the kind of theological critique which has been made many times since then:

> Our religiosity seems to have as little to do with the Christian faith as the religiosity of the Athenians. The "unknown god" [referring to St. Paul's observation in Athens] in America seems to be faith itself. Our politicians are always admonishing the people to have "faith." Sometimes they seem to imply that faith is itself redemptive. Sometimes this faith implies faith in something. That something is usually an idol, rather than the "God and Father of our Lord Jesus Christ," who both judges and has mercy upon sinful men and nations. Sometimes

[12] A. Roy Eckardt, *The Surge of Piety in America* (New York: Association Press, 1958); Will Herberg, *Protestant, Catholic and Jew* (Garden City: Doubleday and Co., 1955); Martin E. Marty, *The New Shape of American Religion* (New York: Harper & Row, 1959); Peter L. Berger, *The Noise of Solemn Assemblies;* Gibson Winter, *The Suburban Captivity of the Churches* (Doubleday and Co., 1961).

we are asked to have faith in ourselves, sometimes to have faith in humanity, sometimes to have faith in America.[13]

This "faith in faith" has been referred to by Martin Marty as America's "fourth faith" [14]—in addition to the faith of Protestant, Catholic, and Jew. It represents a theologically amorphous "religion-in-general" in which God is domesticated into a manageable, cozy deity who is invoked to serve a variety of pragmatic functions of a social, psychological, or patriotic kind. For this very this-worldly, non-demanding cult of religion-in-general, God is the "livin' doll" of Jane Russell's bubbly piety, or the "Man Upstairs" of Roy Eckhardt's analysis.

We will not belabor the description of this generalized, nontheological religion further except to point up the curious paradox which is created by its coexistence with a post-Christian, highly secularized culture. Referring to this as "the paradox of social functionality and social irrelevance," the sociologist Peter L. Berger has described it thus:

On the one hand, organized religion must be functional in American society; otherwise, it could not occupy within that society the place it now has. On the other hand, organized religion is irrelevant to the major social forces which are operative and determinative in American society; it does not affect them, and it relates to them in an overwhelmingly passive way.[15]

The paradox becomes more evident when you compare the tremendous pressures which have been mounted for

[13] *Christianity and Crisis,* January 24, 1955.
[14] *New Shape of American Religion,* ch. 4.
[15] *The Noise of Solemn Assemblies,* p. 38.

the maintenance of a ceremonial observance of religion in the public schools with the widespread abandonment of Christian norms in such areas as sex relationships, business practices, and racial attitudes. What Berger has called "the religious establishment" in America is apparently compatible with a style of life bereft of any distinctively Christian marks. Though it may employ Christian labels and eulogize the idea of a "Christian America," it does nothing to inhibit flagrantly non-Christian practices in public and private life. Faced with this kind of contradictory evidence, a writer like Martin Marty is prompted to raise the question as to whether "the divine-human coziness" of our national religion is not a "theologization" of nihilistic atheism. After all, he observes, "a nonexistent God and a completely captive God are very much alike; under the one or under the other 'all things are permissible.' " [16]

Despite the pretensions of the priests of the cult of religion-in-general, it may be said that America today is largely post-Christian in the sense that the basic patterns of its social, cultural, and political life reflect other than Christian norms. This bespeaks a widespread invasion of the churches by the assumptions of a nonbiblical religiosity. Canon Wedel well describes our plight when he writes: "Our Bible-starved Christianity is in danger of suffering the dread fate of amnesia. We no longer know what we are." [17] In such a situation, it is the task of the theologian to help restore to the church the lost memory of who she is and whom she serves.

There is another sense in which recent writers have

[16] *New Shape of American Religion,* p. 40.

[17] Theodore O. Wedel, *The Gospel in a Strange, New World* (Philadelphia: Westminster Press, 1963), p. 16.

talked about ours as a post-Christian era, however, which poses still another challenge to the churches and their theologians. Many contemporary diagnosticians of the religious scene would echo this observation of John B. Cobb:

In the post-Christian West an ever increasing portion of the population is profoundly estranged from that vision of the world that Christian faith had long made the basis of our cultural common sense. Even among those who self-consciously cling to the Christian faith, many find that the basic vision is fading and that the beliefs associated with it are increasingly problematic.[18]

It is becoming increasingly apparent that the traditional symbols and conceptualizations of Christian faith have lost their compelling and convincing power for many people in our day, and have ceased to be effective vehicles of an "ultimate concern." The problematic nature of traditional theological formulations for many has been dramatically highlighted in recent days by the unusual response to Bishop John A. T. Robinson's book *Honest to God*.[19] However we may evaluate the merits of the book as a theological treatise, the sense of relief and gratitude with which it has been greeted by hosts of thoughtful Christians is a sign of the times which churchmen cannot afford to ignore. It suggests, at the very least, that we can no longer take it for granted that classical theological language, freighted with mythological and metaphysical implications which were meaningful in an earlier historical context, can speak with meaning and relevance to the secularized,

[18] *Living Options in Protestant Theology* (Philadelphia: Westminster Press, 1962), pp. 316-17.

[19] (Philadelphia: Westminster Press, 1963.)

post-Christian man of today, whether he is found inside or outside the churches.

As Robinson sees it, the Christian church is faced today with a crisis of confidence in its means of communication. The crisis is akin to a currency crisis, and it "affects all the traditionally accepted means of exchange among Christians and between Christians and the world in which they live: doctrinal formulations, moral codes, liturgical forms, and the rest." [20] And just as in a currency crisis paper money becomes suspect and people ask for its equivalent in gold or silver, so in our generation people are beginning to ask what, if anything, really backs up these various forms of Christian exchange. What "cash value" in specifiable meaning do our Christian symbols and theological statements really have? What empirical or existential realities are they grounded in and warranted by? [21] "The uneasy suspicion is growing," Robinson concludes, "that churchmen may find themselves holding wads of paper money whose exchange value is virtually nil" and which is convertible only within "the circle of a religious in-group." [22]

This volume is written with the conviction that there are powerful voices among the theologians today capable of speaking prophetically to both aspects of the current crisis which we have been discussing. To the extent to which they are given a hearing, the church will find in-

[20] David L. Edwards (ed.), *The Honest to God Debate* (Philadelphia: Westminster Press, 1963), p. 243.

[21] The two dominant schools of philosophy today, existentialism and analytical philosophy, while diverging radically in method and approach, have both had the effect of pointing the theologian away from abstract metaphysical generalizations to concrete experiential realities as the ground and referent of all theological affirmations.

[22] *The Honest to God Debate,* p. 245.

dispensable resources for its own renewal. Such a renewal must involve at least two things: the arresting and reversal of the process of erosion of the distinctively Christian substance of the church's message and mission; and the finding of new forms for its witness in life and speech which communicate effectively to contemporary secular man. While these are closely related needs and challenges, the first calls primarily for the rediscovery by the church of a vital kerygmatic theology through which it is brought into fresh encounter with the original sources of its faith and life; the second calls primarily for an apologetic theology with the courage to engage in a variety of creative experimentations with new vehicles of expression and communication with the help of which the Christian gospel may be seen again as a live option for twentieth-century man.

Theologians as Prophets

Such resources for renewal are already available to the church in the largely untapped reservoir of prophetic insights still entombed in the massive works of its leading theologians. It may seem a trifle strange to some to cast the theologian in the role of the prophet. The popular stereotype of the theologian as a musty and mystifying character isolated from the toils and tribulations of real life hardly accords with our image of men like Amos and Hosea and their earthly, unambiguous deliverances to the nation of Israel. Stereotypes aside, however, it is not difficult to document the prophetic role of the theologian in our day as in days gone by. We are all familiar with the way in which a fresh articulation of the Word of God, in terms of the idea of justification by faith by a handful of theologians in the sixteenth century, resulted in the profound revolution in the life of the church which we call the Protestant Reformation. Unquestionably, Luther and Calvin were prophets for their day.

In our own day a glowing monument to the theological conviction of the sole sovereignty of God and the exclusive authority of his word in Jesus Christ was raised during the days of Hitler's rise to power in Germany in the declaration of the Barmen Conference of 1934. A group of church leaders, headed by the theologian Karl Barth, had the courage to fling into the teeth of the Nazi tyranny this protest: "Jesus Christ, as he is attested to us in Holy Scripture, is the one Word of God, whom we have to hear and whom we have to trust and obey in life and in death. We condemn the false doctrine that the Church can and must recognize as God's revelation other events and powers, forms and truths apart from and alongside this one Word of God." [23] If it is the task of the prophet to challenge contemporary idolatries, that is a prophetic utterance; and it is of a piece with much theological writing in our time.

It is the function of the prophet to speak for God in the midst of those special moments of crisis in which destiny is decided and issues of eternal import are resolved. It is his awesome task to read the meaning of the *kairos* for his contemporaries. Today the Christian church is passing through just such a *kairos*—a period of her history which is pregnant with danger and opportunity. It is our judgment that God has raised up for such an hour as this prophetic spokesmen within the church, among the ranks

[23] For a full text of the Barmen Declaration, see Arthur C. Cochrane, *The Church's Confession Under Hitler* (Philadelphia: Westminster Press, 1962), Appendix VII.

of her theologians, who are able to assist her in reading more accurately the signs of the times and responding more sensitively to God's particular summons to our generation.

A further mark of the prophet is the resistance and resentment which his message usually provokes on the part of those to whom it is directed. Prophetic voices are usually unwelcome voices, mainly because they jar us loose from customary and hallowed modes of thought and action. They challenge the sanctity of the status quo in matters of belief and conduct. For this reason the church has not been averse to "stoning its prophets." And for this reason, also, the theologian who speaks with a prophetic voice may expect something less than an enthusiastic acceptance from the church which he is endeavoring to serve.

While opposition is in itself no infallible criterion of prophetic truth, the storm of protest which greeted Bishop Robinson's popularization of the views of contemporary theologians may have been the reaction to the sting of a genuinely prophetic thrust. Apparently he, and the theologians he was trying to interpret, had touched an exposed nerve in the church. In any case, the mark of a spiritually mature church should be the ability to read its theologians without rancor, to learn from them even if we may differ from them, and to thank God for every honest attempt to throw new light upon the meaning of his Word for our day. In this connection, there is a statement of Karl Barth's which makes good advice not only for theologians, but for all who encounter theologians more or less at secondhand:

> The theology of every age must be sufficiently strong and free to hear calmly, attentively, and openly, not only the voices of the Church Fathers, not only the voices of its favorites, not

only the voices of classical antiquity, but all the voices of the past in its entirety. . . . For there is always the possibility that in one sense or another we may be in particular need of wholly unexpected voices, and that among them there may be voices which are at first entirely unwelcome.[24]

It is in this spirit that I invite the reader to listen to some of the prophetic voices among the theologians of our time. It may be that there will be among them voices which we would rather not hear because they challenge some of our familiar ways of stating our faith and question some of the traditional forms in which the church has made its witness to the world. Unfortunately, there are those who have their bouts with the Barths, the Bultmanns, and the Bonhoeffers for much the same reason that a prizefighter engages his sparring partners—in order to toughen up their dogmatic muscles and render more inflexible and invulnerable their present theological position. Such a stance can have the unfortunate effect of shackling the freedom of the Holy Spirit in revealing to us truth from unexpected sources and in unexpected ways.

Translating the Theologians

If the church in our day is to be refreshed and renewed by the creative work of its theologians, if the prophetic impact of their ideas is to be significantly felt throughout its life, they must first of all be heard and understood. The new modes of theological understanding and expression which they have been forging must achieve wider currency in the

[24] Quoted by Rudolf Bultmann in the Introduction to Adolf Harnack's *What Is Christianity?* (New York: Harper & Row, 1957), p. ix.

life of the church as a whole, particularly in the thinking and discussions of its ministers and lay leaders.

The anti-intellectualism, to which we referred earlier, is not the only barrier in the way of this wider dissemination of theological understanding. A good deal of the breakdown of communication between the church and its theologians must be attributed to the failure on the part of theologians themselves to write in an idiom which is understandable outside their own professional circle. It is, of course, inevitable that theologians do much of their writing for fellow theologians. And it is as natural and necessary for them as for a scientist to develop a technical jargon that functions usefully as a conceptual shortcut in the discussion of complex and involved issues. But if theology is not to be understood as an interesting language game for theologians but as the self-understanding by the church of its faith and mission, then a way must be found to translate the sometimes esoteric language of the professionals into terms which have real cash value in the life of the church. The first order discussions of the theologians themselves must ultimately produce second order discussions between the theologians and the church if theology is to remain a responsible discipline.

F. Gerald Downing, in his contribution to *The Honest to God Debate,* has used a happy allegory to describe the role which some of us, both ministers and theologians, must play in bridging this communication gap:

> Normally, theological currents pass through many transformer stations before they reach "lay" homes; and in many places, such stations have never been built, or if built, they have fallen into disrepair. And there are many . . . who applaud

this state of affairs, for currents are very dangerous things, and people should be insulated from them, if not by design, then at least by accident. If you try to by-pass the transformer stations you may get a very exciting short-circuit: there is a bright flash, and then all goes dead. On the other hand, you may find many of the lay homes and local churches have all along been wired to stand very high tension indeed, and your dangerous act may by-pass the natural and artificial resistances, and produce a glad and warm light.[25]

While the book *Honest to God* may have been a spectacular short circuit for some, it unquestionably brought a glad and warm light to others whose spiritual and intellectual fuses were capable of handling the high voltage which it carried. The controversial debate which greeted its publication has made one thing clear—the urgency of putting those transformer stations in order so that the vital theological currents of our time may be stepped down for a wider consumption of life-giving insight than the church has yet known.

This task must be assayed at a variety of levels. Theologian, minister, curriculum writer, lay leader—all have a part as they pay the not inconsiderable price of disciplined encounter with the church's great theological minds past and present, and as they wrestle through, sometimes with the sweat, blood, and tears of a profound intellectual and spiritual agony, the deeper and more troublesome issues with which their faith must grapple.

What is called for amounts to (if I may change the figure) a series of theological mining operations in which the precious ore of theological insight is dug out of the

[25] Pp. 126-27.

writings of contemporary theologians and smelted down into a form which can serve as common coinage at least among the more intellectually alert members of the church. It would be presumptuous to think that a task of such magnitude could be accomplished by one man or one book. What the situation calls for is a whole series of attempts to translate and interpret those insights in contemporary theology which are of key importance for the spiritual recovery of the church in our time. This book is offered as one modest contribution to this end.

There is, of course, no dearth of good books about contemporary theologians. But some are more helpful than others in doing the job of translation and interpretation which is needed by the active churchman. Some of the most useful of these have been rather fragmentary pioneering attempts to work out the implications, for the life of the church, of key theological insights of one or more contemporary theologians. Bonhoeffer's thought, for example, has been the main inspiration behind such provocative works as Ronald Gregor Smith's *The New Man* (Harper, 1956); William Hamilton's *The New Essence of Christianity,* (Association, 1961); and Daniel Jenkins' *Beyond Religion* (SCM, 1962). Robinson's *Honest to God* describes the ferment which the thought of Tillich, Bultmann, and Bonhoeffer has occasioned in one responsible churchman's mind and spirit. Arnold B. Come's *An Introduction to Barth's "Dogmatics" for Preachers* (Westminster, 1963) is yet another type of literature designed to make a theologian more useful to the church through the avenue of preaching. There is room for a wide variety of approaches and much creative experimentation in this effort to close the gap, at least at the level of exposition and interpretation, between the church and its theologians.

Our approach in this volume will be to provide a brief introduction to five theologians who more than any of their contemporaries may be said to have broken new ground in the theological work of our generation. There have, of course, been many other prophetic voices among the theologians of the twentieth century. But these five typify those thrusts in the contemporary theological revival which have the most to say to the church at the present critical juncture of her history.

Our treatment of the thought of these men will, of necessity, be highly selective. Many important aspects of their theology will have to be omitted from our discussion in the interests of meaningful concentration. We will, however, attempt to provide sufficient information about the intellectual biography and general theological methodology of each of them to give the reader an appreciation of the uniqueness of their approaches to the theological task. In addition, we will expound briefly those theological themes which in our judgment represent the theologian's most prophetic contribution to the church's self-understanding today. In a concluding chapter we will summarize briefly what seem to emerge from our study as the most promising resources which the theological renaissance has made available for the renewal of the church.

II

KARL BARTH
THE RECOVERY OF BIBLICAL INTEGRITY

Among the prophetic voices raised by the theologians of our time, none has articulated the Christian message more powerfully and reverberated throughout the life of the church more widely than the voice of Karl Barth. By all odds he is the most influential of living theologians. The prophetic impact of his leadership in the German church struggle in the period of Nazi domination has already been noted. That segment of the church in Germany which resisted the idolatry of National Socialism did so largely by the strength of theological convictions given currency by Barth and his followers.

These same theological currents which Barth's fertile mind has continued to generate since World War I have produced the most profound theological revolution of modern times. This revolution has consisted above all in the recovery by contemporary theology of a biblical integrity which had been rather dangerously compromised by both the liberal and fundamentalist wings of the church. The Barthian influence in the theology of our day has challenged equally the liberal dilution of biblical faith by the thought forms of modernity and the orthodox imprisonment of the Word of God in static, infallibly inspired propositions. Steering between the Scylla of liberal accommodationism and the Charybdis of orthodox biblicism, Barth has sought to let the Bible speak for itself, freeing it to address a living, disturbing, and renewing Word to the church. Whatever final assessment is made of the adequacy of Barth's theological formulations as expositions of biblical truth, he must be given the credit for playing a historic role in restoring the Bible to the center of theological discussion in the twentieth century.

Barth's effort to recall theology to a new openness to the Word of God in the Bible has expressed itself in a written product of massive proportions. What was begun nearly fifty years ago as simply a "marginal note" on theology has grown in the intervening years into the most encyclopedic system of theology in the biblical mode since Luther and Calvin. Barth has completed the writing of twelve volumes (nearly one thousand pages each) of his *Church Dogmatics,* and the end is not yet in sight. In addition to this major monument to his theological genius, he has produced forty or fifty smaller books and several hundred articles. Obviously, any attempt to reduce the work of such a prolific writer as this to a chapter summary is an impossible undertaking. In these few pages we can do no more than delineate some of the pioneering thrusts in Barth's thought which have introduced new light and life into the theological dialogue of the twentieth-century church.

"The Strange New World Within the Bible"

The theological revolution which Barth was instrumental in unleashing had its inception in a radical upheaval which occurred early in Barth's own theological development. Barth was born in Basel, Switzerland, the son of a professor of New Testament. Most of his theological studies were pursued in the German universities of Berlin, Tübingen, and Marburg, where he was thoroughly steeped in the thought of the leading liberal theologians of the day, including the neo-Ritschlian scholars Adolf Harnack and Wilhelm Herrmann. Barth was most powerfully influenced by Herrmann, from whom he inherited a brand of Christianity which found its center in the personality of the historical Jesus and the contagious power of his inner religious life as the source of moral transformation.

The theological heritage which Barth took over from his teachers represented the final flowering of influences set in motion by the two towering figures of nineteenth-century theology—Schleiermacher and Ritschl. With these men theology had become oriented in a religionistic and anthropocentric direction. As the result of their work, the Bible tended more and more to be interpreted as a book about man and his religious experiences and moral ideals rather than a book about God and his mighty acts of revelation and redemption. In 1957 Barth identified the weakness of this theology of his student days as follows:

For this theology, to think about God meant to think in a scarcely veiled fashion about man, more exactly about the religious, the Christian religious man. To speak about God meant to speak in an exalted tone but once again and more than ever about this man—his revelations and wonders, his faith and his works. There is no question about it: here man was made great at the cost of God—the divine God who is someone other than man, who sovereignly confronts him, who immovably and unchangeably stands over against him as the Lord, Creator, and Redeemer.[1]

Barth came to see that not only did the religious anthropocentrism with which he began his theological pilgrimage compromise the sovereign otherness of God; neither did it provide a solid enough foundation for the Christian to resist an "uncritical and irresponsible subservience to the patterns, forces, and movements of human history and civilization."[2] This was borne in upon him with disillusioning force when he found to his horror the names of nearly all his theological teachers associated with a manifesto issued in 1914 by ninety-three German intellectuals supporting the nationalistic war policy of the German Kaiser. The shock of this experience convinced Barth of the bankruptcy of nineteenth-century theology and the desperate need for a new theological perspective capable of providing a more adequate basis for the prophetic criticism of society.

The real crisis which forced Barth to a systematic rethinking of his basic theological assumptions, however, grew out of his own personal wrestling with the responsibilities of the preaching ministry. In 1911 he began a ten-year pastorate in the Swiss village of Safenwil. The problem of what to do with the Sunday morning sermon immediately began to plague him. Later he described the nature of the dilemma which confronted him:

I sought to find my way between the problem of human life on the one hand and the content of the Bible on the other.

[1] *The Humanity of God,* pp. 39-40.
[2] *Ibid.,* p. 27.

As a minister I wanted to speak to the *people* in the infinite contradiction of their life, but to speak the no less infinite message of the *Bible,* which was as much of a riddle as life.[3]

This attempt to come to grips with the preacher's problem—what he must say in order to proclaim the Word of God with integrity—has been Barth's preoccupation ever since. As he sees it, theology is by its very nature the servant of preaching. Theology produces the tools of self-criticism and self-examination by means of which the church tests its proclamation of the Word of God.

While there is a place for theology as a specialized activity in the church, no responsible preacher can be content to delegate it to the professionals. Those who heard Barth's recent American lectures will not soon forget his satirical lament about preachers who try to disclaim responsibility for being theologians.

It is always a suspicious phenomenon when leading churchmen . . . along with certain fiery evangelists, preachers, or well-meaning warriors for this or that practical Christian cause, are heard to affirm, cheerfully and no doubt also a bit disdainfully, that theology is after all not their business. . . . And just as bad is the fact that not a few preachers, after they have exchanged their student years for the routine of practical service, seem to think that they are allowed to leave theology behind them as the butterfly does its caterpillar existence, as if it were an exertion over and done with for them. This will not do at all. Christian witness must always be forged anew in the fire of the question of truth.[4]

[3] *The Word of God and the Word of Man* (New York: Harper & Row, 1957), p. 100.

[4] *Evangelical Theology: An Introduction* (New York: Holt, Rinehart and Winston, 1963), pp. 40-41.

It was while Barth was still a parish preacher that he began to raise with great urgency the question of the truth of Christian proclamation. As the grim realities of war rendered increasingly vulnerable his inherited theological position, he devoted himself more and more to an intensive program of Bible study. Comparing notes with Eduard Thurneysen, a close friend who was pastor of a church in a neighboring valley, he began to see the Bible through new eyes. What he called "the strange new world of the Bible" began to open up to him, shattering to bits the bland, man-centered world of his liberal theology.

What is it that confronts us when we are introduced into this "strange new world of the Bible"? In his own words, this is what Barth found: "Not the history of man but the history of God! Not the virtues of men but the virtues of him who hath called us out of darkness into his marvelous light! Not human standpoints but the standpoint of God!" [5] This new theocentric stance became the focal point of Barth's search for biblical integrity in his preaching. In his search he found help also in the Reformers and the much neglected nineteenth-century theologian, Søren Kierkegaard. The results of his accumulated studies finally took shape in a commentary on *The Epistle to the Romans* which was first published in 1918, and again in a revised version in 1921. As Paul Tillich has indicated, this work was "neither a commentary nor a system, but a prophetic call addressed to religion and culture, to acknowledge the divinity of the divine and to dissolve the neo-Protestant synthesis between God's and man's creativity." [6] Its publi-

[5] *The Word of God and the Word of Man,* p. 45.

[6] "The Present Theological Situation in the Light of Continental European Development" in *Theology Today,* October, 1949, p. 302.

cation was an event which shook the theological world with such explosive force that it has never been quite the same since. A much quoted statement in his preface to the second edition shows the radically new direction in which he was moving theologically:

If I have a system, it is limited to a recognition of what Kierkegaard called the "infinite qualitative distinction" between time and eternity, and to my regarding this as possessing negative as well as positive significance: "God is in heaven, and thou art on earth." The relation between such a God and such a man, and the relation between such a man and such a God, is for me the theme of the Bible and the essence of philosophy.[7]

For Barth, at this early stage, the Bible presents us with a "strange new world" because it brings us face to face with a God who is "wholly other." This God is no domesticated, cozy, manageable deity, but a God who in his holiness is incommensurable with anything human. Before God man always stands in a situation of crisis. Between God and man there is a great gulf fixed which can never be bridged from man's side. All such attempts, whether through rational inquiry or religious experience or moral self-justification, are symptoms of man's idolatrous desire to mount up to God on his own terms. Thus, even in his religion—indeed, most especially here—man proves himself to be an enemy of God by his failure to take seriously the radical abyss between the Creator and the creature. But the God of the Bible does not tolerate such creaturely insubordination. He wills to be Lord of his creation, and his divine No thunders forth against man's multifarious

[7] *The Epistle to the Romans* (London: Oxford University Press, 1933), p. 10.

and ingenious attempts to evade his sovereign claim over all life.

Barth was later to acknowledge that this early reaction against his liberal heritage, while a necessary corrective to restore an essential biblical emphasis, was unduly harsh and one-sided. "What should really have been only a sad and friendly smile," he quaintly confesses, "was a derisive laugh!" [8] As we shall see, the sovereignty of God never ceases to be the central theme of Barth's mature theological reflection, though his expositions of it emphasize more and more its gracious rather than its forbidding character, subordinating the divine No of judgment and separation to the divine Yes of electing, reconciling grace.

"God Is Known by God and by God Alone"

The God whom we meet in "the strange new world of the Bible" is the absolutely Sovereign One. His sovereignty is expressed in the very way in which he is known to us. This is the reason why Barth finds revelation to be a crucial category for any theology which pretends to be biblical. An important key to the understanding of his entire theological structure is to be found in a statement which he repeats in one variant or another throughout the *Church Dogmatics:* "God is known by God and by God alone." [9] In this assertion he strikes to the heart of his doctrine of revelation. Everything he says on this topic is designed to insure the absolute independence of the Word of God from human domestication and control, and the sovereign freedom of God in his own revelation so that always "reve-

[8] *The Humanity of God,* p. 43.
[9] CD, II/1, 179.

lation has its truth in the free decision of God." If we are really to let God be God, we must let our knowledge of him be a matter of his disposing and arranging, and not ours. "Who God is and what it is to be divine is something we have to learn where God has revealed Himself and His nature, the essence of the divine." [10]

This fundamental principle has both negative and positive implications. Negatively, it implies that there is in man no natural capacity by virtue of which he can grasp God and make him an object of knowledge. To grant such a capacity would be to put revelation in the control of man and infringe upon the sovereign freedom of God to reveal himself as and where he will. This is the reason why Barth has engaged tirelessly through the years in a running battle against all forms of natural theology which presuppose an analogy between God's being and man's being on the basis of which man can have true knowledge of God quite apart from the grace and revelation of Christ. He views, indeed, the *analogia entis* as "the invention of Antichrist" and the fundamental heresy of Roman Catholicism.[11] It is heretical because it threatens the sovereign initiative of God in his revelation.

For Barth, the opposition to natural theology has been no merely academic issue. He saw it as the life and death issue behind the response of the German church to the challenge of Hitler's idolatry of blood and race. Here the church had to make up its mind whether to allow other "revelations" to insinuate themselves subtly alongside the revelation of God in Christ. Natural theology was the Trojan horse which opened the door to this possibility.

[10] CD, IV/1, 186.
[11] CD, I/1, 4.

If it was admissible and right and perhaps even orthodox to combine the knowability of God in Jesus Christ with His knowability in nature, reason and history, the proclamation of the Gospel with all kinds of other proclamations—and this had been the case, not only in Germany, but in the Church in all lands for a long time—it is hard to see why the German Church should not be allowed to make its own particular use of the procedure.[12]

Barth would undoubtedly diagnose the tendency in some groups in this country to confuse Christianity and good Americanism in much the same way as symptomatic of the encroachment of an implicit natural theology which substitutes our own homegrown idols for the revelation which God himself has given. When asked at his Chicago lectures in 1962 whether the God of a natural theology is always an idol, Barth replied with characteristic directness: "The Bible says so!"

Equally suspect, and for the same reason, is any attempt to find in man "a point of contact" to which Christian preaching could appeal and with which it could link up. God's meeting with man in revelation is not an event which can be facilitated by anything in man "which might be termed a disposition towards the Word of God," Barth insists. "Without any possibility on our side God's great possibility comes into view, making possible what is impossible from our side. It is God's gift, God's free gift, not prepared for by anything on our side, *if* we meet Him and in meeting with Him hear His Word." [13]

Barth's angry controversy with Emil Brunner over the

[12] CD, II/1, 174.

[13] *Dogmatics in Outline* (New York: Philosophical Library, 1949), p. 17.

point of contact [14] took place over thirty years ago. But he is still making the same point today, albeit in milder tones. In his recent little book on preaching he draws out some of the homiletical implications of his position. He takes issue with those who try to justify an extended introduction to the sermon on theological grounds by claiming that "there is in man's nature something that responds to the Word of God and disposes him to hear it." "This might have been true," Barth says, "of Adam in Paradise! . . . But according to the Reformers' understanding of the Bible, there are no such human potentialities; the relationship between man and God is effected from on high by a divine miracle." [15]

So much for the negative implications of Barth's basic premise that "God is known by God and by God alone." What does it imply positively for our understanding of the way in which the miracle of revelation occurs? Barth's view of revelation may be described by the term "actualist," as over against an "intellectualist" view of God's self-disclosure. Revelation is not something at the disposal of man, a permanent deposit of truth which he can possess once and for all and take pride in his possession. Revelation is not in static propositions but in events—events of living divine-human encounter which occur "now and then," "from time to time" (phrases recurring in the *Dogmatics*).

This actualist understanding of revelation as the recurring, dynamic self-disclosure of God in ever fresh apprehensions of faith prevents Barth from making any simple

[14] *Natural Theology*.

[15] *The Preaching of the Gospel* (Philadelphia: Westminster Press, 1963), p. 80.

identification of the Word of God and the Bible, as is done by the fundamentalist. The radically biblical orientation of Barth's theology has led some critics to consign him to the fundamentalist camp. He himself, however, is convinced that fundamentalism or orthodoxy is the third great heresy alongside Roman Catholicism and liberalism. The fundamentalist's literalistic preoccupation with the words of Scripture is a way of freezing revelation and trying to "become master over the Bible, which means master over revelation." [16] Asked by a student, "What differentiates your understanding of the Word of God from that of a fundamentalist?" Barth's reply was, "For me the Word of God is a *happening,* not a thing. Therefore the Bible must *become* the Word of God, and it does this through the work of the Spirit." [17]

This happening of the Word of God takes place in three interdependent forms in the life of the church. The originative, engendering form of the Word of God, upon which the other two forms are based, is the event of God's self-manifestation, once and for all, in Jesus Christ. But this original revelation does not come to us in its naked immediacy. It comes to us through a twofold mediation in the other forms of the Word of God—the witness of Scripture and the proclamation of the church. Apart from these two dependent forms of the Word—the written Word and the preached Word—the living Word, Jesus Christ, never becomes revelation for us.

The function of the written Word is to point beyond itself and witness to Jesus Christ, the primary revelation.

[16] John D. Godsey (ed.), *Karl Barths' Table Talk* (Richmond: John Knox Press, 1962), p. 41.

[17] *Ibid.,* p. 26.

When it does this effectively, when the Spirit quickens in us the response of faith in the apostolic witness to Jesus Christ, the Bible truly becomes the Word of God. "The Bible is God's Word so far as God lets it be His Word, so far as God speaks through it."[18] The Bible in itself cannot be equated with the Word of God in any proper sense. It becomes the Word of God only when it becomes the instrument of a fresh revelation of God. "The Bible therefore becomes God's Word in this event, and it is to its being in this becoming that the tiny word 'is' relates, in the statement that the Bible is God's Word."[19] When by means of the Bible we actually see and hear what the biblical witnesses saw and heard, "where the Word of God is an event, revelation and the Bible are one in fact, and word for word one at that."[20]

In order for the Bible to become the Word of God in the event of revelation, a miracle must take place. The miracle of revelation through the Bible consists in the fact that God speaks through the very human, historically conditioned, and fallible witness of men, but that he really speaks through them. If God's Word is to reach us, it must come through the opaqueness of worldly media which are not themselves the Word of God but veil the Word of God. As far as the Bible is concerned, this opaqueness includes such things as the fallibility of the biblical writers with respect to historical judgments, and even their capacity for religious and theological errors. As a genuinely human word the Bible is highly vulnerable, and "only the

[18] CD, I/1, 123.
[19] *Ibid.*, p. 124.
[20] *Ibid.*, p. 127.

miracle of faith and the Word can genuinely and seriously prevent us from taking offence at the Bible."[21]

It is in preaching as contemporary witness to the Word that this miracle takes place again and again in the life of the church. When preaching becomes a true witness to the word of the apostles which in turn was a witness to the Word of God in Jesus Christ, it becomes itself a third form of the Word. It is in this proclamation, indeed, that the church finds its only reality and continuity. "The Church is constantly going forward to this happening of proclamation. The Church is always becoming the Church. It is always being reformed. It lives in *remembering* and *expecting,* between past and future proclamation."[22] The faltering human words of the preacher can again and again be the instrument of a fresh revelation of God, as God chooses to use them. The possibility of this happening in the future as it has in the past is what invests the preaching situation with tingling expectancy. And in this possibility lies the hope for the continued renewal of the church as it responds in fresh acts of obedience to a living, contemporary Word of God.

The Good News of God's Humanity

What is the content of this Word by which the church is continually sustained and renewed? The thousands of pages of Barth's *Church Dogmatics* are eloquent, if wordy, testimony to his profound conviction that the message which the church has to proclaim is unambiguously good news. It is pure gospel. No theologian has outdone Barth

[21] CD, I/2, 507.
[22] *Karl Barth's Table Talk,* pp. 25-26.

in the consistency with which he has elaborated a theological perspective in which grace is the dominant and all-controlling theme. For him the gospel is one grand symphony celebrating the incomprehensible wonder of God's grace. As a matter of fact, the very style and structure of his theological writing resembles more a symphonic composition than a logical system. Election, creation, reconciliation, redemption—in Barth's hands these theological concepts are but different ways of expounding, developing, and recapitulating, often in subtle and intricate subthemes, the one great affirmation of God's gracious act of redemption in Jesus Christ.

One is not surprised to find a theologian with such an obsessive preoccupation with the grace of God nicknamed "God's joyful partisan." [23] When Barth visited the United States in 1962 many Americans found that the nickname fitted the man as well as his theology. The irrepressible good humor, the earthy playfulness, the infectious joy which radiated from the man seemed utterly consonant with his conception of theology as "the most thankful and *happy* science!" [24] Shattered forever was the stereotype of Barth as the "gloomy theological gladiator and fire-eater" which had long been entertained in this country on the basis of the angry polemics in which he used to indulge in the days of his commentary on Romans.

As we have seen, in the early days Barth was concerned to burn into the consciousnes of a complacent Christendom the truth of the deity of God which puts everything human under a vast question mark. "We viewed this 'wholly

[23] The title of an article on Barth in a German newsmagazine, *Der Spiegel,* on December 23, 1959.

[24] *Evangelical Theology: An Introduction,* p. 12.

other,' " Barth today acknowledges, "in isolation, abstracted and absolutized, and set it over against man, this miserable wretch—not to say boxed his ears with it—in such fashion that it continually showed greater similarity to the deity of the God of the philosophers than to the deity of the God of Abraham, Isaac, and Jacob." [25]

The mature Barth stresses no less emphatically than before the deity and sovereignty of God. But he now defines God's deity in terms of his humanity. So defined, God's sovereignty is seen not in the exercise of some abstract omnipotence, but in his freedom to be for man instead of against him, his freedom to choose man as the eternal object of his love, his freedom to be man's servant and brother as well as his Lord and King. "Who God is and what He is in His deity He proves and reveals not in a vacuum as a divine being-for-Himself, but precisely and authentically in the fact that He exists, speaks and acts as the *partner* of man, though of course as the absolutely superior partner." [26]

This, then, is the unbelievably good news which has been entrusted to the church for its proclamation—the humanity of God. But how do we know it to be true? As an abstract truth which might be suspected of being merely a human postulate or speculation, it would be something less than the triumphant gospel to which the biblical writers consistently bear witness. The glowing certainty and unadulterated joy of the apostolic testimony to the humanity of God has only one explanation—the conviction that here we are not dealing with a general truth which might or might not be true, but with a concrete act

[25] *The Humanity of God,* p. 45.
[26] *Ibid.*

of God in history through which he has visited and redeemed his people and in which we know him as Immanuel —"God with us." For this concrete confrontation with God's humanity there is only one name—Jesus Christ.

This is the reason for the so-called christological concentration throughout the whole of Barth's theology. "There are strictly speaking," he says, "no Christian themes independent of Christology, and the Church must insist on this in its message to the world." [27] God in his freedom has chosen to declare and define his relationship to man and the world in Jesus Christ. No theologian or preacher has the right, therefore, to look elsewhere than to him for the basis and justification of all his speaking about God. Every Christian affirmation about man as well as God, about creation as well as redemption, about ultimate beginnings as well as final destiny, gains its truth and certainty only as it fits into "this basic and determinative pattern, model and system," [28] which is set forth in God's gracious uniting of himself with our humanity in Jesus Christ. The following quotation gives some indication of the thoroughgoing way in which Barth elucidates the entire spectrum of Christian doctrine in christological terms:

Between God and man there stands the person of Jesus Christ, Himself God and Himself man, and so mediating between the two. . . . In Him God stands before man and man stands before God, as is the eternal will of God, and the eternal ordination of man in accordance with this will. In Him God's plan for man is disclosed, God's judgment on man fulfilled,

[27] CD, II/1, 320.
[28] CD, II/2, 8.

God's deliverance of man accomplished, God's gift to man present in fulness, God's claim and promise to man declared. In Him God has joined Himself to man. And so man exists for His sake. It is by Him, Jesus Christ, and for Him and to Him, that the universe is created as a theatre for God's dealings with man and man's dealings with God. The being of God is His being, and similarly the being of man is originally His being. . . . He is the decree of God behind and above which there can be no other, since all others serve only the fulfilment of this decree. . . . He is the election of God before which and without which and beside which God cannot make any other choices. . . . For it is God's free grace that in Him He elects to be man and to have dealings with man and to join Himself to man.[29]

If Jesus Christ is the touchstone of all Christian truth, he is this because he is the fulfillment in history of a primordial decision of God made before history began. Barth is prepared to assert that Jesus Christ, the God-man, existed eternally as the concrete content of God's eternal decision to enter into a partnership of love with all men. For this reason the doctrine of election is no peripheral addendum to theology, but its central presupposition. It is the articulation of that which makes the gospel genuinely good news. "The doctrine of election is the sum of the Gospel because of all words that can be said or heard it is the best. . . . Its function is to bear basic testimony to eternal, free and unchanging grace as the beginning of all the ways and works of God." [30]

There is a way of thinking about election, of course, which leaves man's destiny so ambiguous that it is any-

[29] *Ibid.*, pp. 94-95.
[30] *Ibid.*, p. 3.

thing but good news. Such is the traditional Calvinist doctrine of double predestination according to which a certain number of men are marked from eternity for salvation and a certain number of others for damnation. The gospel, as Barth sees it, however, is not in this way "a mixed message of joy and terror, salvation and damnation." [31] We can be triumphantly certain about God's eternal decision concerning us, because it is not a decision cloaked in some hidden "absolute decree" but one which has been made gloriously manifest in Jesus Christ. If we wish to know with assurance who is the electing God and who is the elect Man, we must look to him and to him alone.

What does the event of Jesus Christ tell us about the content of God's eternal decision? It assures us that from the beginning God has determined to humble himself by becoming man in order that man might be elevated to covenant partnership with himself. The condescension of God and the exaltation of man both take place in Jesus Christ, who is true God and true man. In the history of his divine humanity he is the miracle of our reconciliation with God. "Man's reconciliation with God takes place through God's putting Himself in man's place and man's being put in God's place, as a sheer act of grace." [32] The wonder of this "great exchange" lies in the fact that in it the No of God's judgment against man's sin is answered decisively, and once and for all, by his Yes of forgiving love. In the cross he bears the bitter fruit of man's rejection, while in the resurrection he is raised to a place of honor at God's right hand, the eternal victor over sin and death. The inconceivable marvel of this gracious substitu-

[31] *Ibid.*, p. 13.
[32] *Dogmatics in Outline*, p. 115.

tion is that it is Jesus Christ as God who chooses for himself the suffering and humiliation, while it is Jesus Christ as man who is chosen for the glory of eternal fellowship with the Father.

This sovereign act of God's reconciling grace has decisive implications for all men, whether they realize it or not. God's victory in their behalf has already been won. The death blow against their sin has already been struck. And in the humanity of Jesus they have already been claimed as objects of God's undying love and marked for resurrection and glory. No amount of sinful resistance can undo what has been done. "The war is at an end—even though here and there troops are still shooting, because they have not heard anything yet about the capitulation." [33] In this light sin is shown up for what it is as sheer impotence, futility, and irrationality.

Does this mean universalism—the view that all men will be ultimately saved? Although the logic of his position would seem to lead in this direction, Barth refuses to give an unequivocal answer to such a question. While he believes "that we have no theological right to set any sort of limits to the loving-kindness of God which has appeared in Jesus Christ," [34] neither do we have the right to limit the freedom of God by insisting that he *must* save all men. At the same time he confesses puzzlement at those "whose most pressing problem seems to consist in this, that God's grace in this direction should be too free, that hell, instead of being amply populated, might one day perhaps be found to be empty." [35]

[33] *Ibid.,* p. 123.

[34] *The Humanity of God,* p. 62.

[35] Quoted by Robert M. Brown in the introduction to Georges Casalis' *Portrait of Karl Barth* (Garden City: Doubleday and Co., 1963), p. 20.

That grace is God's first work as well as his last word for man is the daring affirmation of the Christian doctrine of creation. The cosmic proportions of the Christian understanding of salvation can be truly grasped only when creation itself is seen as an act of grace and an instrument of God's covenant of grace with man. Barth resists any suggestion that the work of our salvation and redemption might be "a kind of afterthought which we might ignore in view of creation as God's first and principal work." [36] No. Jesus Christ is Alpha as well as Omega. This means that the covenant concluded in him was God's intention *before* he created the world and man. Creation, then, is not a neutral sphere of God's activity which can be made meaningful in itself, apart from Christ, as a sort of prehistory which precedes the history of redemption. Creation took place solely with a view to Jesus Christ as the stage upon which would be played out the history of God's gracious dealings with man. The created world has its existence and meaning only in the fact that it is a theater of redemption, a realm of reality which God has posited outside himself and upon which he can lavish his love.

Only when creation is thus seen in its inner connection with the covenant is it possible to affirm its essential goodness and declare it to be pure benefit to the creature. The Christian who views God's act of creation in accordance with the model of his act of reconciliation in Jesus Christ cannot avoid seeing it also as a triumph of divine grace. This is the only proper context, Barth insists, for understanding the mystery of the presence of evil in God's universe. Evil is that which God does not will. It is therefore what God passed over and rejected when he created the

[36] CD, III/1, 46.

world. "He rejected the reality of a creation that might be neutral or hostile to Him. He pushed it back and outside the limit of the world willed and determined by Him." [37] As such, it has no positive reality in the world which God has made. And yet it has its own kind of problematic being. "It 'is,' not as God and His creation are, but only in its own improper way, as inherent contradiction, as impossible possibility." [38] Its reality is the reality of that which God in creation "passed over and set aside, marking and excluding it as the eternal past, the eternal yesterday." [39]

Thus, on the basis of creation as well as reconciliation and election, Barth is a "Christian optimist." For him there is no place for the category of the tragic in Christian thinking about the world. Nor is there any place for the note of melancholy in Christian preaching. To be sure, existence has its shadow side because it borders on the realm of chaos and nothingness. But the sadness and sorrow of life cannot quench the indomitable faith of the Christian that in Jesus Christ God has intervened to conquer decisively the power of nothingness and evil, rendering it forever impotent; and that this triumph of grace is foreordained in his eternal decree and prefigured in the very fabric of creation itself.

Barth finds in Mozart the best musical exponent of these joyous theological convictions which lie at the heart of the gospel which the church is privileged to proclaim. Mozart is Barth's "food and drink." Each day begins for him with a playing of one or two Mozart recordings. Better than

[37] *Ibid.*, p. 102.
[38] CD, III/3, 351.
[39] *Ibid.*, p. 353.

even the theologians of the church, Mozart was able to communicate through his music a vision of "creation in its total goodness." [40] In this music there is shadow as well as light, the threatening No as well as the triumphant Yes; but the former is always enclosed within and finally subordinated to the latter. Here, then, is music free from both cloying sentimentality and unresolved doubt and certainty. That is why it is such a matchless vehicle of creation's praise to God, joyously hymning the sovereignty of the Creator's grace in all that he has made.

God's Freedom and Ours

We have seen that, for Barth, God's freedom is expressed concretely in his humanity, that is, in his freedom to choose man in and through Jesus Christ. Because of that choice, grace is the first and last word we must say about God. And because of that choice, man is determined in his very being for God. On the basis of the reconciling work of Christ every man, whether he knows it or not, is marked and pledged for covenant partnership with God.

What does this leave for man to do? In what way does his freedom enter into the determination of his destiny? It is at this point that the most persistent criticisms of Barth's theology have arisen. Many have felt that in his zeal to magnify the grace of God, Barth has not made adequate provision for the decisive role which human freedom must play in the appropriation of salvation. In John C. Bennett's expressive phrase, here is a theology in which man is virtually "swamped by grace." Moreover, everything seems to have been determined in advance in an *a*

[40] *Ibid.*, p. 298.

priori decision of God in eternity in such a way as to evacuate the decisions of history of any positive significance. The result would seem to be, as Emil Brunner has observed, "that the real decision only takes place in the objective sphere, and not in the subjective sphere." [41]

These kinds of criticism raise real questions about the adequacy of Barth's theological perspective at certain crucial points. It is significant to note, however, that if Barth errs, he does so not as so many have done by cramping and confining the scope of the gospel, but by giving it the most generous possible interpretation. "Most of Barth's problems," Robert M. Brown has reminded us, "are raised because he gives such total credence to all that is joyous and liberating in the Christian message." [42]

Moreover, it would be a mistake to conclude that for Barth the human response to God's gracious activity is theologically superfluous. This is abundantly evident in the lengthy discussions of ethics after each of the four major sections of his dogmatics—election, creation, reconciliation, and redemption (the last two yet to be completed). This arrangement reflects Barth's conviction that the task of theology is never finished till the implications of its central concepts for man's life in the world are worked out. A theology of the Word of God must necessarily raise the ethical question at every level of its discussion simply because its object is "the Word of the living

[41] *The Christian Doctrine of God, Dogmatics, Vol. I* (Philadelphia: Westminster Press, 1950), p. 351. Cf. also Arnold B. Come, *An Introduction to Barth's "Dogmatics" for Preachers,* ch. V, for a remarkably acute criticism of the tendency of Barth's Christomonism to relativize history, absorb humanity into God, empty faith of positive content, and unduly limit the mission of the church.

[42] *Portrait of Karl Barth,* p. 32.

God addressed to the living man absorbed in the work and action of his life."

Therefore dogmatics loses nothing more nor less than its object, and therefore all meaning, if it is not continually concerned as well with the existence of man and the realities of his situation, if its problem concerning the purity of doctrine and the Word of God in Christian preaching is not also the problem of the Christian life of man, i.e., the life of man as determined by the Word of God: the problem what we ourselves must do.[43]

The answer to this "existential" question as to what we must do as addressees of God's eternal word of grace can be summed up, Barth says, in a single word: gratitude. "If the essence of God as the God of man is His grace, then the essence of men as His people, that which is proper to and demanded of them in covenant with God, is simply their thanks." [44] To give thanks in word and act and being —this is the all-embracing content of man's response to a covenant-making God. This encompasses everything which is required of him. This is his destiny—to echo gratefully in the concrete decisions of his daily life the gracious decision which God has made for him in Jesus Christ. This is his true humanity—to be and to do in each moment of his existence what will reflect, acknowledge, and confirm God's sovereign work of grace as Creator, Reconciler, and Redeemer.

In this approach to theological ethics, the ethical imperative arises out of and is inseparable from the evan-

[43] CD, I/2, 792.
[44] CD, IV/1, 42.

gelical indicative. This means that the law which commands our obedience is implicit within the gospel which frees us for that obedience. "Ruling grace is commanding grace. The Gospel itself has the form and fashion of the Law. The one Word of God is both Gospel *and* Law." [45] As gospel, the Word of God speaks of God's being and action in creation, reconciliation, and redemption. As law, it speaks of man's responsibility to conform to God's being and action by the joyful acceptance of his vocation as God's creature, partner, and child.

Since the law is the form of the gospel, the imperative implied in grace, the Christian ethic must be first and foremost an ethic of freedom. It has nothing to do with a law which threatens and harasses and robs him of his essential freedom. The joyless, compulsive legalism which has too frequently been characteristic of the teaching of the church is utterly foreign to the ethics of grace and gratitude as found in the New Testament. The command of God does not enslave man, but sets him free. It does this by summoning him to his true humanity, to the realization of the inner law of his being as one destined for covenant relationship with God.

Barth is at pains to distinguish this "freedom of the Christian man" from the alleged freedom represented by a neutral "free will" capable of choosing either good or evil. "God does not put man into the situation of Hercules at the crossroads," says Barth. Such a situation in which man has freedom to choose wrongly as well as rightly can only mean bondage. "Man becomes free and is free by choosing, deciding, and determining himself in accor-

[45] CD, II/2, 511.

dance with the freedom of God. . . . Trying to escape from being in accord with God's own freedom is not human freedom."[46] Barth sees man's sinful attempts to reject God's gracious lordship of his life as a vain bid for a freedom inconsistent with God's freedom which does nothing but land him in a morass of enslaving compulsions. "When man sins . . . he is delivered up, like a hunted beast to the hounds, to what the world and life and men want of him, to what above all, he himself must continually want of himself."[47] In God's world, the world marked by the victory of his grace in Jesus Christ, this so-called freedom to sin can have no ultimate standing. It is an "ontological impossibility," an absurd episode in man's history which God has from the beginning branded as an impotent lie. The only real freedom open to man is the freedom of glad and grateful obedience to the divine commands which issue from the heart of the gospel.

In what way do the commands of God come to us? In answering this basic question of ethics, Barth reflects the same actualist presuppositions which we found to be operative in his doctrine of revelation. The divine imperative always lays hold of us as an event. It is not summed up for us in a set of rules or distilled in a general program valid for the whole of life or embodied in fixed principles to be applied to particular situations by the best methods of casuistry which our human ingenuity can devise. The living Word and Will of God cannot be frozen in any of these ways in permanently congealed molds. The content of the divine command must be discovered anew in each situation in fresh encounters between the free God and the

[46] *The Humanity of God*, pp. 76-77.
[47] CD, II/2, 586-87.

free man. It is always apprehended as a quite specific form of obedience. "Man will be and actually is told what is good and what the Lord requires of him—and with absolute definiteness, so that only obedience or disobedience remains, and there is no scope for his free appraisal and will in regard to the shape of his obedience." [48]

The knowledge of what it is that God wills for us in this or that situation does not, of course, spring forth from a vacuum. This insight is generated from a continuous encounter with the Word of God as witnessed to in Scripture. On the basis of the testimony of the biblical writers as to what the divine command was there and then, we are made aware of what it is for us here and now. This does not mean we are able to consult it as a box of magic cards from which we can mechanically read off the content of our Christian obligation in a given situation. "Therefore the Bible is the source and norm and judge of all ethical disciplines, not as a pack of cards, not as it is divided and dissolved into a multiplicity of timeless revelations of the divine will unrelated to history, but in the historical unity of its content." [49]

Thus, the Bible will not direct us to the commands of God in a legalistic fashion. The weakness of legalism is its failure to do justice to the uniqueness of the historical situation as it affects the shape of Christian obedience. Within the "historical unity" of biblical testimony specific commands of God are discernible which are normative for

[48] CD, II/2, 704. John C. Bennett has raised what would appear to be a legitimate question about the false impression Barth gives of "the degree of unambiguity that is possible in our discerning of God's command," in a review of *Church Dogmatics,* III/4 in *Union Seminary Quarterly Review,* November, 1962, p. 74.

[49] CD, II/2, 705.

the Christian today. But Barth again and again makes room for exceptional cases in which God requires something which may depart from the central norm. Thus, for example, the indissolubility of marriage is commanded; but divorce may be permitted in special instances where a marriage is seen not to represent the will of God. Or, to take another example, suicide is a frustration of the will of the Creator, and therefore prohibited; but if a man has good reason to believe that under torture he may betray his friends, the taking of his own life may be justified.

In this attempt to identify the specific content of Christian faithfulness, the individual is never left to his own devices. In the discussions of the Christian community, past and present, there are signposts which can help point him to the proper use of his Christian freedom. The process of mutual counseling within the fellowship of the church may be the event through which God in his freedom chooses to utter his word of command. In the final analysis, however, no other human being can answer for us the question as to what constitutes Christian obedience in any situation. This is a matter of an individual decision which faithfully mirrors God's decision. For this reason, Christian ethics "leaves the uttering of the essential and final word to God Himself." [50] Only in this way can God's freedom as well as ours be honored in each decision.

The Word of God and the Renewal of the Church

The freedom of Christian decision can be assured only by a continuous openness to the Word of God so that every answer we give to the question of what constitutes Chris-

[50] *The Humanity of God,* p. 88.

tian obedience is genuinely contemporary and not a form of enslavement to what we or others have decided in the past. Past answers must ever and again be opened up for fresh scrutiny in the light of what God may be saying to us today from his Word. Herein lies the secret of renewal in the life of the church. In a key passage Barth identifies the renewal which issues from the free and recurring encounter with the Word of God as the law of the church's life:

> The Church is most faithful to its tradition, and realises its unity with the Church of every age, when, linked but not tied by its past, it to-day searches the Scriptures and orientates its life by them as though this had to happen to-day for the first time. And, on the other hand it sickens and dies when it is enslaved by its past instead of being disciplined by the new beginning which it must always make in the Scriptures. . . . The principle of necessary repetition and renewal, and not a law of stability, is the law of the spiritual growth and continuity of our life.[51]

This statement typifies the signal contribution of Barth's work to the theological self-understanding of the church in our day. That his theology is open to criticism at various points does not denigrate the greatness of his achievement in recalling us to a new fidelity to the Word of God addressed to us in Scripture. We may take issue with his sometimes fanciful exegesis of certain scriptural passages, particularly in the Old Testament, in which their obvious meaning is unduly stretched to make them fit into his christological framework. We may wonder at his reluctance

[51] CD, II/2, 647.

to admit specific cases of fallibility in the Bible, despite his general denial of its inerrancy. We may question whether his bold, detailed descriptions of what transpires in the inner life of the Godhead do not take him beyond the data of biblical revelation into the realm of extra-biblical, philosophical speculation against which he has fought so vehemently. Finally, we may share the suspicion of theologians like Bultmann and Tillich that Barth's wholesale rejection of the apologetic dimension of theology seriously impairs the effective communication of the gospel to the outsider in our secular age.

These and other difficulties in Barth's thought may prevent us from becoming Barthians. But they should not dull our appreciation for the inspiring way in which he has challenged the church of our day to a radical dependence on the source of its life and the dynamic of its renewal—the Word of God. Each of the theologians to be considered in subsequent chapters builds in his own way on this basic foundation of biblical integrity which Barth has secured for the theology of our times. Barth has left us all in his debt by forcing us to do what he himself has done—"to listen afresh to Scripture in the life of the church, not to reinforce a Barthian theology but to see how and in what ways the Word of God is speaking a fresh, challenging, upsetting and yet ultimately renewing word to the church and thereby to the world." [52]

[52] *Portrait of Karl Barth,* pp. 2-3.

III

RUDOLF BULTMANN THE SEARCH FOR THE RIGHT SCANDAL

Between the two world wars the name of Karl Barth effectively dominated the European theological scene. By mid-century, however, the center of gravity in theological discussion had noticeably shifted. Returning from a visit to Europe in 1952, Paul Tillich had this to say: "When you come to Europe to-day, it is not as it was before, with Karl Barth in the centre of discussion; it is now Rudolf Bultmann who is in the centre." [1] Tome after tome of Barth's *Church Dogmatics* have, to be sure, continued to flow from the presses in an awesome proliferation of theological verbiage. But the questions increasingly exercising continental, and to a somewhat lesser degree American, theologians have had their source in Bultmann rather than Barth. While much current theology can be classified as post-Bultmannian, it is still wrestling with issues and problems which Bultmann projected to the center of the theological stage.

Rudolf Karl Bultmann was born in 1884, the son of an Evangelical Lutheran pastor. Among his theological teach-

[1] Quoted by John Macquarrie, *The Scope of Demythologizing* (New York: Harper & Row, 1960), p. 13.

ers were the eminent liberal scholars of the day, Rudolf Harnack, Johannes Weiss, and Wilhelm Herrmann. The bulk of his teaching career, from 1921 to 1951, was spent at Marburg. Here he was for a time a colleague of the existentialist philosopher Martin Heidegger, whose thought has influenced so deeply the conceptual framework into which he has endeavored to recast the Christian faith.

Bultmann and Barth

When Bultmann was first making a name for himself in the theological world, he was usually classified along with Barth as a member of the new movement of "dialectical theology." As Barth has increasingly turned away from his earlier reliance upon the existentialism of Kierkegaard, and as Bultmann has more and more appealed to the existentialism of Heidegger, the gap between the two has progressively widened. Bultmann has been unwilling to repudiate his early heritage of liberalism as decisively as has Barth. Indeed, his work may be seen as an effort to construct a new synthesis between elements of value in liberalism and neo-orthodoxy. This interpretation of the significance of his theological labors is confirmed in an autobiographical statement written in 1956:

It seemed to me that . . . the new theology had correctly seen that Christian faith is the answer to the word of the transcendent God that encounters man and that theology has to deal with this word and the man who has been encountered by it. This judgment, however, has never led me to a simple condemnation of "liberal" theology; on the contrary, I have endeavored throughout my entire work to carry further the tradition of historical-critical research as it was practiced by the "liberal" theology and to make our more recent theological knowledge fruitful for it.[2]

Bultmann first gained worldwide recognition for his work in New Testament studies, particularly his development of the method of form criticism originated by his teacher, Johannes Weiss. The use of this method of studying the New Testament documents led to a rather extreme skepticism about the possibility of recovering an accurate picture of the Jesus of history with which liberal theology had been so preoccupied. According to Bultmann and his fellow form critics, the Gospels are not so much biographical accounts of the life and teaching of Jesus of Nazareth as expressions of the faith of the early church. They represent the church's attempt to interpret, in line with its teaching and preaching needs, the significance of Jesus' life and death as a saving act of God in history. They are to be read, not as objective sources of historical knowledge concerning what Jesus actually did and said, but for insight into what the early Christians believed about Jesus and the forms in which their faith was expressed in the message which they proclaimed to their contemporaries.

These conclusions, arrived at on the basis of historical criticism of the Bible, were highly compatible with the theology of the Word of God being propagated at the same time by Barth and his followers. Gone was the concentration on the personality and teachings of the historical Jesus as the basis of the Christian faith which had been characteristic of theological liberalism. Now in the center of

[2] Schubert M. Ogden, (ed.), *Existence and Faith, Shorter Writings of Rudolf Bultmann* (New York: Meridian Books, 1960), p. 288.

theological discussion was the kerygma—the message of God's mighty act of salvation centering in the cross and resurrection, and its challenge to decision and commitment.

In their concern to identify and expound this New Testament kerygma, Bultmann and Barth stand on common ground in opposition to the older liberalism. It is in their estimate of what it takes to make the content of the kerygma intelligible to modern man that they come to a parting of the ways. Bultmann sees the need for much more drastic measures than Barth to extricate the gospel from its first-century setting and make it accessible to men today. For his part, Barth is fearful that the program of demythologizing and existential reinterpretation, which Bultmann sees as a necessary means to this end, may result in a return to the "Egyptian bondage" to philosophy from which theology has been so recently delivered.

The False Scandal of Myth

As Bultmann sees it, the modern church is confronted with an unprecedented crisis in communication. He shares with the Neo-Reformation movement in theology an emphasis upon the scandal which confronts men in the proclamation of the New Testament kerygma. He endorsed Barth's rediscovery of "the strange new world of the Bible." But Bultmann has long been haunted by the suspicion that modern preaching has too often confronted men with the wrong kind of "strangeness" in the Bible. He would agree with Paul Tillich that there are, after all, two kinds of "stumbling blocks" which men can face in their encounter with the Bible—one legitimate and one illegitimate.

Tillich has suggested that the wrong stumbling block is erected by our inability to communicate the gospel effectively so that men can decide for or against the real thing. "What we have to do is to overcome the wrong stumbling block in order to bring people face to face with the right stumbling block and enable them to make a genuine decision." [3]

It is this essentially apologetic purpose—to remove the wrong stumbling blocks and to search out and define as unambiguously as possible the true scandal of the biblical message—which has been the major motivation in Bultmann's lifework. His is the concern not alone of an academic theologian and New Testament scholar, but also of a preacher of the gospel who is vitally involved in the task of getting the Christian faith across to modern men in terms in which it may be understood. His unusual sensitivity to this problem is evident when one reads his sermons, one volume of which has been published in English.[4]

David Cairns, in a commentary in which he grapples with the significance of Bultmann for the preacher, speaks appreciatively of his gift of sensitiveness to what the auditors of his sermons may be thinking:

As you read his sermons, you can hear the question which is in the back of his mind: Supposing there is a man who has just come into this church; a man with little or no religious background; how much of all this that I am saying will have any meaning to him? As he listens to me, is he all the while saying

[3] *Theology of Culture* (New York: Oxford University Press, 1959), p. 213.

[4] *This World and the Beyond* (New York: Charles Scribner's Sons, 1960).

to himself, "Try as I may, I simply cannot believe that"? Or is he quite unable to attach a meaning to my words? Do they seem to him pure myth, or even worse, mumbo jumbo? [5]

As Bultmann sees it, when modern men sit down and try to read the Bible and make sense of it, it turns out to be just that—mumbo jumbo! And so he has explicitly addressed himself in his theological work to the problem of twentieth-century man who finds the first-century setting of the Bible strange and remote from the understanding of the universe which he has come to accept on the basis of modern science. He is concerned about the multitudes in our day who do not reject the Bible with any intelligent understanding of what it is that they are rejecting, but who pass it by, as it were, by default, because they cannot make head nor tail of the mythological framework in which so much of it is cast.

It is Bultmann's belief that the New Testament kerygma is couched in so much mythical language that it is virtually meaningless for many people today. Our task, he says, is to set free the essential New Testament proclamation of God's saving act in Jesus Christ from the dated and largely unintelligible language and thought forms of the ancient world so that today we can be genuinely addressed by it and decide for or against it.

This is not to remove the scandal and offense of the gospel. It is simply to remove the wrong occasion for stumbling over it. The gospel does not require of us a sacrifice of the intellect by forcing us to accept a view of the world in the realm of our faith which we deny in our everyday life. If men are to turn their backs on the Bible

[5] *A Gospel Without Myth?* (London: SCM Press, 1960), p. 15.

and reject God's gift of new life in Christ, it should be for the right reason; not because they are in the position of the Ethiopian eunuch before Philip joined him in his chariot and was unable to decipher sacred Scripture for want of an interpreter, but because like the rich young ruler they understand all too well the implications and demands of the gospel and reject it because they are unwilling to pay the price of commitment.

Bultmann's proposals for demythologizing the New Testament were first set forth in his famous programmatic essay "New Testament and Mythology" [6] which was published at the height of World War II in 1941. Its publication set off an immediate chain reaction among German theologians, stimulating one of the most spirited debates in the history of modern theology.[7]

Bultmann was by no means the first theologian to draw attention to the problem of myth in the New Testament. But his essay was unique in the uncompromising rigor with which he drew the issues and pointed up their crucial significance for the life and health of the church. It was a clarion call to "absolute clarity and ruthless honesty" among both theologians and pastors concerning what is essential in the Christian faith. His challenge to them was pointed:

It is a duty they owe to themselves, to the Church they serve, and to those whom they seek to win for the Church. They must make it quite clear what their hearers are expected to

[6] H. W. Bartsch, (ed.) *Kerygma and Myth* (Torchbook ed., New York: Harper & Row, 1961), pp. 1-44.

[7] Five volumes of essays replying to Bultmann's thesis have been collected and edited by H. W. Bartsch, some of which originally appeared only in mimeographed form because of limitations imposed by the war.

accept and what they are not. At all costs the preacher must not leave his people in the dark about what he secretly eliminates, nor must he be in the dark about it himself.[8]

In the opening passage of his essay, Bultmann paints a vivid picture of the mythological world view which the biblical writers take for granted, but which when preached today presents men with a false scandal. Here is a portion of that description:

The cosmology of the New Testament is essentially mythical in character. The world is viewed as a three-storied structure, with the earth in the centre, the heaven above, and the underworld beneath. Heaven is the abode of God and of celestial beings—the angels. The underworld is hell, the place of torment. Even the earth is more than the scene of natural, everyday events, of the trivial round and common task. It is the scene of the supernatural activity of God and his angels on the one hand, and of Satan and his daemons on the other. These supernatural forces intervene in the course of nature and in all that men think and will and do. Miracles are by no means rare. Man is not in control of his own life. Evil spirits may take possession of him. Satan may inspire him with evil thoughts. Alternatively, God may inspire his thought and guide his purposes. He may grant him heavenly visions. . . . History does not follow a smooth unbroken course, it is set in motion and controlled by these supernatural powers. This aeon is held in bondage by Satan, sin, and death (for "powers" is precisely what they are), and hastens towards its end. That end will come very soon, and will take the form of a cosmic catastrophe. It will be inaugurated by the "woes" of the last time. Then the Judge will come from heaven, the dead will rise, the last

[8] *Kerygma and Myth,* p. 9.

judgment will take place, and men will enter into eternal salvation or damnation.[9]

All this is typical, says Bultmann, of the mythological framework in which much of the New Testament is cast. Mythical ways of speaking also extend to descriptions of the person and work of Christ in the use of such notions as preexistence and virgin birth as ways of interpreting his significance for the faith of the early Christians. But these mythical conceptions in which the New Testament gospel was originally conveyed must be rejected in their totality as a false scandal today.

Bultmann advances a number of reasons why he considers some form of demythologizing imperative for us in the modern proclamation of the gospel. For one thing, most of the mythological trappings which surround the message of the New Testament can be shown to have nothing specifically Christian about them. As a biblical scholar, he purports to be able to trace their origins to either the Jewish apocalyptic writings or the redemption myths of gnosticism.

Not only do they represent the vestigial remains of an obsolete world view, but for modern man they are altogether incredible. In a day in which "all our thinking is shaped irrevocably by modern science," it would be quite arbitrary to demand a blind acceptance of New Testament mythology. Indeed, it would be a way of denying the Reformation doctrine of justification by faith, for it would require us to offer up to God a kind of works—the works of sacrificing and suppressing the intellect and forcing it insincerely into "accepting a view of the world in our

[9] *Ibid.*, pp. 1-2.

faith and religion which we should deny in our everyday life." [10]

Despite his deference to what the scientifically oriented man of our day is able to swallow intellectually, Bultmann disavows any motivation "to make the New Testament relevant to the modern world at all costs." [11] The most urgent imperative for demythologizing is the evangelical purpose of laying bare the real challenge of the gospel and enabling us to achieve the understanding which the New Testament writings themselves intend.

The basic intention of the myths of the New Testament is to express a certain understanding of human existence as grounded in and limited by a transcendent divine power. When they are interpreted literally as objective events in nature and history, they actually falsify the nature of God and his relation to the world. "It may be said," Bultmann writes, "that myths give to the transcendent reality an immanent, this-worldly objectivity. Myths give worldly objectivity to that which is unworldly." [12] Thus, for example, God is represented as inhabiting a localized heaven to which Christ literally ascends when he leaves his disciples for the last time and from which he returns on the clouds at the end of the age. Bultmann sees evidence of an awareness in New Testament writers themselves of the inadequacy of such mythological conceptions when interpreted literally. In the later writings of Paul and John the process of demythologizing begins within the New Testament itself. In John, for example, you find the

[10] *Ibid.*, p. 4.
[11] *Ibid.*, p. 10.
[12] *Jesus Christ and Mythology* (New York: Charles Scribner's Sons, 1958), p. 19.

earlier mythological eschatology replaced by a conception of eternal life as a reality already present in the life of the believer.

Finding the Right Scandal: The Hermeneutical Question

So much for the problem. Now what does Bultmann propose as a solution? Given the fact that the myths of the New Testament confront men today with a false stumbling block, what then are we to do with them? Are we simply to jettison them, assuming that they have nothing important to say to us, yielding up no authoritative truth for our lives in the twentieth century? No, emphatically not, says Bultmann. This was the way taken, by and large, by liberalism, and Bultmann will have none of it. He rejects the road taken by his teacher Harnack, for example, who tried to strip away the "husk" of biblical religion—its mythical and theological paraphernalia—in order to lay bare its essential "kernel." But what was left when he had finished the "peeling away" process was only a handful of general principles of religion and ethics such as the kingdom of God, the infinite worth of the soul, and the commandment of love. Gone entirely was the kerygma, the triumphant message of the early church of a decisive act of God for man's redemption.

Bultmann has been influenced too deeply by Barthian ways of thinking to play fast and loose in this way with the New Testament kerygma. For him it is axiomatic that "the New Testament speaks of an *event* through which God has wrought man's redemption." [13] To be sure, this

[13] *Kerygma and Myth,* p. 14.

event is set forth by the New Testament in mythological terms. But this does not mean that we can dismiss the myth as irrelevant, as if it did not enshrine within it a gospel. However meaningless the mythological conceptions of the New Testament may be for us today as far as their objective features are concerned, they nevertheless embody a meaning which has redemptive significance for men in every age.

All this means, then, that demythologizing for Bultmann does not involve an outright rejection of the myth, but an interpretation of it—an interpretation which is so related to our own experience that it calls for a genuine decision on our part. He has himself reminded us that at bottom "*de-mythologizing is an hermeneutic method,* that is, a method of interpretation, of exegesis." [14] Hermeneutics may be defined as the study of the principles and methods of interpretation according to which the meaning of ancient texts are made accessible to contemporary understanding. In no small measure because of the impetus of the demythologizing debate, the hermeneutical question has become perhaps the most burning single issue in recent theological discussion.[15]

Basic to Bultmann's hermeneutical method is his use of the insights of existentialist philosophy, particularly the philosophy of Martin Heidegger, as a conceptual framework for communicating the deeper meaning of the biblical message to modern man. In this use of a particular philosophy he does not feel that he is imposing something

[14] *Jesus Christ and Mythology,* p. 45.

[15] For a recent contribution of Emil Brunner's successor, Gerhard Ebeling, and others to this discussion see James M. Robinson and John B. Cobb, Jr. (eds.), *The New Hermeneutic* (New York: Harper & Row, 1964).

foreign upon the New Testament, because he is of the conviction that both existentialism and the New Testament are appealing to the same basic understanding of human existence. They are both trying to challenge men to an authentic kind of human existence in which they take responsibility for their own lives without flying for refuge in false securities.

Before we proceed to examine Bultmann's use of existentialist insights to expose the true scandal of Christianity, it will be helpful to look more closely at his reason for invoking the aid of existentialist philosophy as a hermeneutical tool. According to Bultmann, no text—be it the Bible, a scientific treatise, or a piece of poetry—can be understood and interpreted according to the intention of its author without asking of it the right kinds of questions. When we interpret any piece of literature, we do so in terms of certain presuppositions as to what the appropriate questions are for which it affords answers. The particular questions we ask are rooted in a "life relation" which we have with the subject matter of the text, and a "preunderstanding" implicit in this life relation without which the meaning of the text would be completely closed to us. As an example, for most people a book on advanced astrophysics is likely to be completely opaque to them because they lack the life relation with the subject with which it deals and the necessary preunderstanding to enable them to interrogate it meaningfully and thus unlock its esoteric secrets.

Bultmann is convinced that despite the handicap of the mythological form in which much of its message is couched, the Bible need not be in this way a closed book to modern man. For he has, as men have always had, the necessary life relation with and preunderstanding of the subject matter of the Bible to enable him to ask of it the right questions by means of which it is made to yield up its essential meaning.

The crucial question then becomes: What is the right kind of question to address to the Bible in order to elicit its true meaning?

The lamentable history of the conflict between science and religion is a monument to the dangers inherent in asking the wrong questions of the Bible. Confusion is bound to result, for example, as long as we expect the Bible to answer questions of scientific fact. What kind of question, then, is it proper to bring to the Bible? Bultmann answers that "the question which is appropriate to the Bible is the question about human existence—a question to which I am driven by . . . the question of my own existence." [16] This means that the Bible is potentially meaningful to every man, because every man is absorbed in the question of the meaning of his own life, a question which is inseparable from the question of God.

This, then, is the fundamental insight which the myths of the New Testament are trying to convey (though as myths they do it inadequately); they are trying to communicate a certain understanding of human existence in relation to God. The task of the theologian in demythologizing is to exhibit their existential meaning by showing the understanding of human existence which is implicit within them.

At this point, the philosophy of existentialism becomes relevant to the theological task, as Bultmann sees it. If the central intention of the Bible is to confront us with a

[16] Quoted from Macquarrie, *The Scope of Demythologizing,* p. 41.

choice between alternative understandings of our existence, then it is part of the theologian's job to show that these self-understandings are in fact real possibilities for human beings. If this is not done, the biblical message remains mere myth and is incapable of addressing us with a genuine option for our real existence.

In his efforts to show that it does present us with a live option, the theologian of today can find enormous assistance, Bultmann believes, in the philosophy of existentialism. It is the merit of this particular brand of philosophy to concentrate its attention on a systematic analysis of the most general structures of human existence. In other words, the existential analytic provides us with a set of concepts which are descriptive of the possibilities which are open to the mode of being called man, for which Heidegger coins the term *Dasein*. If the theologian can show that the particular understanding of human existence which faith affirms in the New Testament is consistent with this conceptualization of the structures and possibilities of *Dasein* generally, he has made a real decision for the Christian self-understanding possible. He has shown, moreover, that the revelation of God is not something utterly foreign, thrown into human existence and violating the intelligible call of God to man to the realization of genuine possibilities of his being as man.

The Content of the Christian Scandal: The Challenge to Authentic Existence

Now we are in a position to see how Bultmann uses the tools of existentialist analysis as provided by Heidegger to clarify the Christian understanding of sin and salvation, which is the real scandal with which modern man must be confronted.[17]

Heidegger analyzes two basic structures which are possibilities for human existence wherever it is found. He calls them *inauthentic existence* and *authentic existence*. Bultmann suggests that the New Testament writers, and Paul in particular, make a similar distinction when they contrast the life "according to the flesh" with the life of the Spirit, the life apart from faith with the life of faith. When we understand what is involved in the transition from the one to the other, we know what is meant by salvation in the Christian sense. While the nature of this transition is understood differently by the existentialist philosopher and the Christian, the conceptual framework which Heidegger uses to describe authentic and inauthentic existence can be used by the theologian to clarify what it is we are saved from and what it is we are saved to. Thus our understanding of salvation is grounded in concrete possibilities of human existence and disentangled from the mythological references which sometimes make the New Testament language of salvation confusing to modern man.

Let us look first, then, at what it is that Christian faith affirms we are *saved from* as this is illuminated for us by Heidegger's concept of inauthentic existence. In very general terms, man falls into inauthentic existence when he becomes so merged with and enslaved by the world that he loses his authentic being in the process. Thrown into existence in a world which is fundamentally alien to his

[17] I am indebted in this section to John Macquarrie's excellent comparative study of the thought of Heidegger and Bultmann in *An Existentialist Theology* (London: SCM Press, 1955).

being, endowed with the freedom to be a real self over against this world, man feels threatened and anxious. He is tempted to allay this anxiety by surrendering himself to the world and immersing himself in its being, thus giving up the vocation of being an authentic self. When this happens he becomes involved in what Heidegger refers to as the structure of "fallenness" (*Verfallenheit*).

Fallenness is experienced by man in two different ways corresponding to the inauthentic ways of "being-in-the-world" and "being-with-others." The inauthentic mode of being-in-the-world is characterized by an exclusive preoccupation with things. In this expression of fallenness man desperately attempts to establish his own security by the mastery of things but ends up by being mastered by them. He tries to understand the meaning of his life solely in terms of the disposable, objective world; but the more he succeeds, the more he ceases to be a real self.

This inauthentic mode of being, Bultmann says, is described theologically by the apostle Paul through his use of the term "flesh" (*sarx*). In his characteristic usage, Paul speaks of life "after the flesh" as a turning from the Creator to the creature, an attempt to ground one's life in those visible, earthly securities which are disposable and controllable by man. Thus the flesh, as Paul uses the term, does not refer primarily to biological existence as such, but to a way of life in which man can indulge in boasting of a man-made security, taking confidence in the flesh rather than in God. In this sense the spirituality of the Jewish legalist is as fleshly or carnal as the sensuality of the profligate, for both of them are striving to find meaning for their threatened existence in terms of visible, tangible, man-made realities.

There is an inauthentic way of being-with-others as well as being-in-the-world. In his analysis of this type of fallenness Heidegger has given us some fascinating characterizations of the ills which plague our modern depersonalized society. In this inauthentic way of being-with-others, the self ceases to take responsibility for its own existence and turns it over to what Heidegger calls *das Man,* or "the public." The public, which is men-in-general but no-one-in-particular, thus becomes the omnivorous dictator to which the self defers in all matters of taste and judgment and decision. This capitulation of the self results in such things as "everydayness" or mediocrity, the dissipation of the self in baseless talking and scribbling which caters to popular tastes without regard to truth, and the curiosity which looks for vicarious thrills in the escapades of movie stars and public figures. Such devices are all ways in which the inauthentic self seeks to rid itself of the weight of its own existence and avoid the dread necessity of personal decision.

How is this mode of fallenness described in the New Testament? Bultmann sees it expressed in the Pauline and Johannine concept of the world (*cosmos*). This word is typically used in the New Testament not in the cosmological but the existential sense. That is, it refers to the sphere of human relations, specifically to man as a corporate entity. It is a concept at least roughly analogous to Heidegger's public, suggesting a transpersonal social power which tyrannizes over individuals who are said to be dominated by "the spirit of the world," and subject to "the prince of this world" or "the god of this world." The New Testament at times resorts to mythological ways of speaking of these things in order to describe the hostile character of the world. But in Bultmann's existential interpretation, the hostility of the world derives not from quasi-personal demonic forces, principalities and powers, but from man's own decision to allow himself to fall into bondage to the world of things and other people.

The ultimate consequence of fallenness is the falling away of man from himself, that is, alienation from his authentic existence. Having scattered his being in the world of things and the world of the anonymous public, he has lost the power to be himself. While Heidegger's analysis does not include any reference to God, it is a short step indeed to the Christian concept of sin as alienation from God. Paul was very much aware of the way in which sin represented an alienation of man from his authentic self. In the seventh chapter of Romans he expresses this very clearly: "It is no more I that do it, but sin that dwelleth in me." Paul's real "I," his authentic self, was no longer in control; it was displaced by "sin," the structure of an inauthentic existence to which he was in bondage as to a strange "law" which warred against his real self. In being alienated from this authentic self, he was also alienated from God who had created that self. Thus "the carnal mind," the mind which understands its existence in an unauthentic way, "is enmity against God."

With the help of the existential analytic, Bultmann has tried to give content to the idea of sin as a concrete possibility of human existence. He has done the same with the doctrine of salvation. Salvation, in brief, is the emancipation made possible through Jesus Christ of those who are held in bondage to the structures of inauthentic existence. It is the actualization of a new understanding of man's life on the basis of his authentic self. It is thus the restoration of the original possibilities of his being as a creature made in the image of God. As such it does not involve a magical and mysterious transformation of man's substance but the realization of possibilities which were there from the beginning but which man in his sinful inauthenticity had lost.

The New Testament writers describe authentic existence with a variety of terminology. Sometimes it is referred to simply as "life." "I am come that they might have life, and that they might have it more abundantly." Sometimes it is called life after the spirit in contrast to life after the flesh. But such descriptions of the saved life, Bultmann insists, must be understood existentially rather than substantially. In other words, salvation is not a matter of a transfusion into man by the Holy Spirit (at baptism or at the time of conversion) of some kind of substance which alters his ontological nature. It is rather a matter of having opened up for him new concrete possibilities of authentic existence. It is the gift of freedom to be his real self.

This freedom is many-sided. It is, first of all, freedom from the world. The man of faith participates in the world, but he does so with an inner distance and detachment from the world as if he did not. So Paul exhorts the Corinthians: "Let they that have wives be as though they had none; and they that weep, as though they wept not; and they that rejoice, as though they rejoice not; and they that buy, as though they possessed not; and they that use this world, as not abusing it: for the fashion of this world passeth away" (I Cor. 7:29-31). Thus the authentic life of faith frees a man from frenzied attachment to all earthbound securities and commits him to live by the strength of the invisible and uncontrollable in complete reliance upon God.

Authentic existence means also deliverance from our past and freedom for the future. An experience of the grace of God assures us of the forgiveness of sins and creates in us the "faith that the unseen, intangible reality actually confronts us as love," releasing us from our past guilt and enabling us "to open ourselves freely to the future." This means freedom for obedience while "giving up every attempt to carve out a niche in life for ourselves, surrendering all our self-confidence, and resolving to trust in God alone." [18] In the following excerpts from one of his sermons Bultmann describes the way in which the faith of the Christian endows him with a certain nonchalance about the future:

> Hence the Christian does not allow his life to be determined by a self-chosen aim, to which all his energies and hopes are bent; but his life is rather characterized, in a certain sense, by lack of specific aim, by which we mean an inner freedom from self-chosen aims. The faith of the Christian is that the future will bring him his true self, which he can never capture by his own self-appointed courses. In other words, readiness for my fate, for that which God designs to do with me.[19]

The Basis of Authentic Existence: The Christ Event

This then is the true scandal with which the modern preacher should burden his listeners—the challenge to

[18] *Kerygma and Myth,* p. 19.
[19] *This World and the Beyond,* p. 78.

forsake their inauthentic mode of living and embrace the authentic life of faith. The full dimensions of the scandal are not apprehended, however, until it is realized that this transition cannot be brought about by man on his own power. It is at this point that Bultmann parts company with existentialism and, as John Macquarrie suggests, sets a "limit to demythologizing." [20]

For Heidegger, the transition to authentic existence is made by man's own resolve in answer to the call of conscience. Conscience awakens man to his authentic self in the midst of his fallenness, and on the basis of this awareness he is able to recover his true self in detachment from the world. Bultmann, on the basis of the more radical estimate of the extent of man's fallenness found in the New Testament, denies that such self-salvation is a possibility for man. The existentialist philosopher can, indeed, conceive of what authentic existence would be like, but he is unable to realize it in his own experience apart from the saving act of God in Christ. In this appeal to the kerygma, the proclamation of the Christ event as the necessary precondition of salvation, Bultmann prevents his theology from being dissolved into existentialism.[21]

How does Bultmann conceive of this act of God without which authentic existence is unattainable? He describes it

[20] *The Scope of Demythologizing*, p. 11.

[21] It should be pointed out that some of Bultmann's left-wing disciples have refused to follow him at this point in calling a halt to demythologizing. Fritz Buri on the continent and Schubert Ogden in America have, in effect, dekerygmatized as well as demythologized the New Testament by their denial that a unique act of God in Christ is essential for salvation. Cf. Schubert L. Ogden, *Christ Without Myth* (New York: Harper & Row 1961), p. 144: "Not only is it *possible* to affirm that authentic existence can be realized apart from faith in Jesus Christ or in the Christian proclamation; it is, in fact, *necessary* that this affirmation be made."

as the eschatological event—the event which inaugurates the new age—the event which frees man for a new life. "It makes a man free from himself and free to be himself, free to live a life of self-commitment in faith and love." [22] The Christ event has the power to do this because it grounds our confidence in the love of God in something more solid than wishful thinking. It is because the Christ event is above all else a revelation of God's love that it can provide the only possible basis for authentic existence: "Only those who are loved are capable of loving. Only those who have received confidence as a gift can show confidence in others. Only those who know what self-commitment is by experience can adopt that attitude themselves." [23]

The Christ event which mediates this love and self-comment of God to us is grounded in the once-and-for-all past action of God in the cross and resurrection. It becomes a saving event for us, however, only through the present proclamation of the church, as we participate in it through the decision of faith. Thus the saving significance of the Christ event does not stem from its character as an event of past history; nor does it lie in some mythologically understood cosmic transaction between God and Christ or between Christ and Satan; but in its challenge to us to "make the cross of Christ our own" and participate in "the power of his resurrection," in a word, to decide for authentic existence.

The most problematic item on Bultmann's demythologizing agenda for many people is his treatment of the resurrection. He insists that the resurrection is "the

[22] *Kerygma and Myth,* p. 32.
[23] *Ibid.,* pp. 32-33.

eschatological event *par excellence.*" [24] It is such, however, not as an objective historical phenomenon of the same order as the crucifixion, but as a mythological representation of the meaning of the cross. "Indeed, *faith in the resurrection is really the same thing as faith in the saving efficacy of the cross,* faith in the cross as the cross of Christ." [25] All that the historian can be sure of, as far as the event of resurrection is concerned, is the Easter faith of the early disciples. It is this Easter faith, according to which the cross is interpreted as a saving act of God rather than a human tragedy, which is proclaimed in Christian preaching. It is this that men are called upon to accept in the decision of faith, not belief in the resuscitation of a dead body.

For Bultmann, the Christ event is not complete apart from the preaching of the church and the faith-response to that preaching. As an event of past history, divorced from its contemporary appropriation by the faith of men and women, it has no saving efficacy whatsoever.[26] As a truly eschatological event, in which the grace of God apprehends us in the preaching of the cross, it must be renewed again and again in ever fresh decisions of faith. Eschatological existence is not a permanent condition in which the believer can comfortably rest upheld by the objective

[24] *Ibid.*, p. 40.

[25] *Ibid.*, p. 41.

[26] At this point Bultmann differs decisively from Barth, for whom, as we have seen, the saving work of Christ has an objective, cosmic significance as a supernatural fact which is efficacious quite apart from its subjective appropriation by the believer. Emil Brunner has recently criticized both the "extreme objectivism" of Barth and the "extreme subjectivism" of Bultmann from the standpoint of his theology of encounter. Cf. his section on "Theology Beyond Barth and Bultmann" in *Truth as Encounter* (Philadelphia: Westminster Press, 1964), pp. 41-50.

securities of a doctrine or a written word. An alleged experience of salvation which is not renewed by the constant, moment-by-moment decision of faith is an escape into inauthenticity, rather than the gift of authentic human existence. At this point, Bultmann's theology is a powerful antidote against the pious protestations of those who claim they are saved on the basis of a childhood act of faith, but whose present mode of life bears no evidence of the renewal of that faith in the marks of authentic Christian freedom.

Demythologizing and Renewal

It has not been my purpose in these pages to debate the merits of Bultmann's particular solutions to the problem of myth in the New Testament and the theological reconstruction to which they lead. A voluminous literature exists which has tackled this task from a variety of perspectives. Most of his responsible critics have suggested that he either went too far or did not go far enough in his demythologizing project. Only extreme conservatives have condemned the demythologizing enterprise as such.

Among those who recognize the basic validity of Bultmann's undertaking, some feel that he has carried demythologizing, particularly with respect to the question of miracle, much further than is needed in the interests of coming to terms with the modern scientific outlook.[27] Others, as we shall see in our study of Tillich, question whether the gospel can be translated into existential statements as exhaustively as Bultmann seems to suppose without risking the loss of essential elements in the Christian message which can be expressed, in the final analysis, only

[27] Cf. Cairns, *A Gospel Without Myth*, ch. VI.

in mythical terms. Still others, such as John A. T. Robinson,[28] believe that, in his capacity as a New Testament critic, he relegates too much of the history of the Gospels to the status of myth because of an unwarrantably radical historical skepticism.

These criticisms, however, do not in any way devalue the vital importance of Bultmann's contribution in dramatically pinpointing an issue which has enormous implications for the renewal of the church in our time. If Barth's gift to the church—the recovery of the centrality of the Word of God—is to be preserved in the secular milieu of our day, we must take seriously Bultmann's challenge to come to grips honestly with the problem of myth in the Bible. Increasing numbers of people within the church (to say nothing of those outside it) are quite at a loss to know what to do with passage after passage of scripture which is heavily weighted with mythical descriptions. And in their quandary, they are tempted to throw out the whole business as having nothing vital to say to the real world in which they live and the vexing problems with which they must grapple. It would be interesting to know how many sincere and thoughtful people in the churches have reluctantly abandoned the reading of their Bibles because of the false stumbling block of myth.

The problem of understanding is complicated by the fact that the term "myth" is so laden with negative emotional overtones. Those who do not understand the way in which the theologian employs the term jump to the conclusion that to call something a myth is simply to label it as untrue fiction. Hence they immediately react defensively against

[28] Cf. *Honest to God,* p. 35.

the suggestion that large parts of the Bible are mythical. Only when they are made to see that the designation myth says nothing whatsoever about whether something is true or false are they prepared to consider the problem of mythology in the Bible without prejudice. Only then is it possible to see that myth in the Bible may represent a peculiar kind of truth—the truth of a picture language which expresses in story form the theological significance of certain events and realities.

There is, of course, room for honest differences among Christians as to how much of the biblical narratives, e.g., the stories of Jesus' birth, resurrection, ascension, and second coming, are to be regarded as myth, in the sense just described, and how much as factual history. But that some discrimination between the two be clearly made is essential to the integrity of the church's proclamation. To continue to present the myths of the Bible to modern man as if they were history is to put him off by a false scandal. And, as Bishop Robinson has warned, "By failing to differentiate and assess the mythological positively for what it is, we *cause* him to relegate biblical narratives to a fairy-story world which has no connection with our history at all." [29]

In his search for the right scandal in the Christian faith, Bultmann may not have exhausted all the possibilities of meaning in the biblical myths. But his concentration on the existential meaning of biblical language has done much to explode the notion that Christian doctrines are intellectual antiques to be collected and preserved by those who have an interest in such things, but which have little

[29] *The Honest to God Debate,* p. 267.

relevance for the real business of life in the world. He has shown the crucial importance of "cashing" Christian beliefs by drawing out their implications for concrete human existence.

If the church is to be renewed in our day, Christian beliefs must somehow "come alive" in some such way as Bultmann has tried to make them. The doctrine of sin must be seen as the self-made bondage of Everyman to the tyranny of worldly securities, rather than the poisonous legacy of a mythical first man. The doctrine of salvation must be seen as God's gift to us of authentic freedom to be our true selves in service to others, rather than the working out of some cosmic plan of redemption to which we are called upon to give our intellectual acceptance. Similarly, we cannot really claim belief in the cross of Christ without taking up our own crosses and following him; nor in his resurrection without exhibiting the power of a new life. And finally, we can articulate most convincingly our belief in the kingdom of God, not by our ability to recite a timetable of events for the Last Day, but by living constantly in "the dimension of the eternal," in momentary expectation of God's breakthrough into our lives in grace and judgment.

When Christian doctrine has been translated into such existential terms as these, the search for the right scandal in the Bible has met at least with some degree of positive fulfillment.

IV

PAUL TILLICH
BOUNDARY LINES AND BRIDGES

Paul Tillich occupies a unique position in contemporary American theology. With the publication of the third and final volume of his *Systematic Theology* in 1963, the most influential work of any systematic theologian in this country in the twentieth century came to an impressive culmination. Born the son of a Lutheran pastor in Germany in 1886, Tillich spent the early part of his career teaching philosophy and theology in German universities. In 1933 his criticism of the Hitler regime resulted in his dismissal from a professorship at the University of Frankfurt. Under the sponsorship of Reinhold Niebuhr, he was invited to join the faculty of Union Theological Seminary in New York, where the bulk of his creative work as a theologian took place. After his retirement from the Union faculty in 1955 he served at Harvard University and the Divinity School of the University of Chicago.

In addition to his *Systematic Theology,* which had been in the making since 1925, Tillich's thought took shape in a steady stream of books and articles on a great variety of themes. Few problems of religious and theological thought escaped his penetrating and illuminating analysis. He succeeded, as few men in modern times have done, in bringing together in a remarkably creative and original synthesis insights from many widely divergent movements both past and present. His theological position represents the confluence of the classical tradition of Greek and medieval philosophy, the mystical and idealist strains in nineteenth-century thinkers like Schelling and Schleiermacher, the existentialism of Kierkegaard, and the basic understandings of Reformation and Neo-Reformation theologians. The profundity and complexity of the system which emerges from this massive effort at synthesis defies easy interpretation and assimilation. In this chapter we can hope only to scale a few of the foothills of the mountain which must be climbed in any attempt to come to grips with Tillich's thought.

Theological Bridge Building and the Method of Correlation

According to his own confession, Paul Tillich was destined to live out his life both personally and professionally "on the boundary." Just to tick off some of the boundary lines which he occupied gives you the picture of a man with a tremendous catholicity of concern who spent a lifetime relating the Christian faith creatively to wide areas of human thought and experience. Here are some of them: the boundary between faith and doubt; the boundary between philosophy and theology; the boundary between the Old World and the New World; the boundary between Christianity and culture (particularly psychology and art); the boundary between Christianity and other religions; the boundary between Protestantism and Catholicism; the boundary between apologetic and kerygmatic theology; the boundary between liberalism and neo-orthodoxy.

Such a boundary line stance represents both peril and opportunity. It makes him exceedingly vulnerable to the criticism of those who are deeply entrenched on one side of the boundary or the other. For those who like to take their dogmas straight, Tillich's thought is profoundly suspect. By the same token, it stands in judgment upon all narrow provincialisms which erect Berlin Walls of the mind and the spirit to choke off free intellectual commerce with their neighbors. Where some theologians specialized in wall-building, Tillich devoted his energies to bridge-building. The result has been to breathe new vitality and relevance into many of the traditional formulations of Christian theology.

While their theology differs in important respects, Tillich has been driven by the same overarching concern as Bultmann to make the Christian faith a live option for modern man. This is evidenced in an impassioned remark he once made at a meeting of the American Theological Society in defending his position against certain criticisms. As reported by W. Norman Pittenger, he said:

> The whole reason for my work is that I want to make Christian faith possible for the people of our time. I think always of the young men and women in our universities who would be Christians; yes, I think of young men in our seminaries who lie awake at night worrying because they cannot honestly become what they want to become; and I am trying to make this Christian theology mean something for them and help them understand what it is saying and why it is saying it.[1]

[1] "Paul Tillich as a Theologian: An Appreciation" in *Anglican Theological Review,* July, 1961, p. 268.

And despite a vocabulary sometimes overfreighted with the obscure terminology of the classical tradition of philosophy, he had remarkable success in doing just that—communicating the gospel with particular effectiveness to the intellectuals of our day.

It would be a mistake, however, to dismiss Tillich as simply an apostle to the intellectuals—those twentieth-century "cultured despisers" of religion who flocked to hear him by the thousands on the campuses of colleges and universities across the country. His thought has rich resources also for the preachers and teachers of the church who are concerned with the task of restating the gospel with freshness and relevance for our times. Three published volumes of sermons, gripping in their simplicity and spiritual perception, attest to the effectiveness with which his thought is capable of being aimed at the problems of the man in the pew.[2]

Before we proceed to a discussion of some of the more substantive themes of Tillich's theology, we need to get before us a general picture of his theological method and his understanding of the nature of religious symbolism, which is so decisive in shaping his formulation of doctrinal conclusions. To these matters we now turn.

The very way in which Tillich structured his theology insures that the apologetic concern is dominant throughout. In the preface to his *Systematic Theology,* he states that his purpose is "to present the method and the structure of a theological system written from an apologetic point of view and carried through in a continuous correla-

[2] *The Shaking of the Foundations* (New York: Charles Scribner's Sons, 1948); *The New Being* (Charles Scribner's Sons, 1955); *The Eternal Now* (Charles Scribner's Sons, 1963).

tion with philosophy." [3] This does not mean that he fails to take revelation seriously; every theologian works within what he calls a "theological circle" which is the result of his commitment to a special revelatory experience. It does mean that in the "method of correlation" which Tillich adopted, the theological answers which are implicit in the revelation are systematically worked out by the theologian in correlation with the existential questions which emerge from the human situation. The theologian's grasp of this situation is greatly enhanced by taking seriously the concrete descriptions of it in the art, literature, and philosophy of his day.

The failure of both fundamentalism and Barthian kerygmatic theology lies in their ignoring in their theological work this concrete situation into which the gospel must be received. Fundamentalism does so by trying to speak "from a situation of the past." Barthianism does so by denying any real point of contact between the Christian faith and man's cultural activity and thought, throwing the gospel, as it were, at men's heads "like a stone." Tillich maintains that this approach is impossible

> because the revelatory answer is meaningless if there is no question to which it is the answer. Man cannot receive an answer to a question he has not asked. . . . Any such answer would be foolishnes for him, an understandable combination of words—as so much preaching is—but not a revelatory experience.[4]

The implicit indictment of much contemporary preaching contained in this statement has far-reaching prophetic

[3] (Chicago: The University of Chicago Press, 1951), I, vii.
[4] *Systematic Theology* (The University of Chicago Press, 1957), II, 13.

significance for the church today. The accelerating drift away from organized Christianity may be traceable more than we think to the failure of Christian preaching to be informed by a truly "answering theology."

There are those who have charged that Tillich's use of the "method of correlation" led him in his theology to purchase relevance at the price of compromising the substance of the Christian answers. This may be true. But it is hard to see, if it is true, how it is a necessary outcome of his method. Tillich is well aware that any theological method is subject to distortion, but he believes that the method of correlation is as self-corrective as any. In insisting on the independent importance of both the existential questions and the theological answers, it forestalls any attempt to derive the answers from the human situation itself, as was the temptation in liberal theology; at the same time it discourages the arrogance of the theologian who pretends to be able to pull the answers out of his sleeve without any real wrestling with the anguished questions which emerge from man's existential predicament.

While the theologian works within a circle which is defined for him by his particular faith commitment, this circle is actually more like an ellipse with two centers representing the existential question and the theological answer. The *substance* of question and answer must be kept separate and not be allowed to prejudge each other. The *form* which each of them takes within the theological system, however, will be dependent upon each other. For the theologian, as a man of faith, will inevitably shape the questions posed by human existence in such a way that they reflect not only the theologian's profound empathy with the realities of the human predicament, but also his awareness of the kind of answers which theology provides for them. Similarly, the theological answers will be formulated in such a way as to exhibit their relevance to the real questions which men are asking out of the depth of their existence. We will see, later in the chapter, the way in which this formal interdependence of question and answer is illustrated in Tillich's treatment of the doctrine of salvation as he correlates man's existential estrangement with the New Being in Jesus as the Christ, and in his treatment of the doctrine of the church as he correlates the ambiguities of life and religion with the Spiritual Community which embodies the New Being. Before we do this, it will be helpful to examine his understanding of the nature of religious language, especially his views of symbol and myth and their bearing on how we are able to think and speak of God.

The Problem of How to Speak of God: The Language of Ultimate Concern

It is a basic conviction of Tillich's that all religious language is necessarily symbolic. This means that every theological answer which revelation provides for the questions arising out of the human predicament inevitably takes the form of symbolic statement. Why is this so? Because the language of faith is always the language of an ultimate concern. And since it is trying to say something about the ultimate, that is, about the infinite ground of our being and all being, it is bound to fall short of being literally adequate to describe the inexhaustible mystery of which it speaks. This is why all our language about God must be oblique language, employing symbols drawn from our this-worldly experience which are incapable of expressing directly or literally the transcendent reality to which they point.

At this point Tillich always anticipates such a question as this: "What! Do you mean the Christian faith is only a bunch of symbols?" To which he always replies that the objection "only a symbol" is a surefire symptom that the objector does not understand what a symbol is. Specifically, he has failed to see the difference between a symbol and a sign. The chief difference lies in the fact that while both symbols and signs point beyond themselves to something else, only symbols participate in the reality to which they point. Signs serve their pointing function as a result of more or less arbitrary conventions, as when we agree to allow a red light to point to the meaning "stop." Signs can always be changed when we find it expedient to do so. It is always possible, for example, to have a blue light do service for a stop sign as long as we make clear to all concerned that we are changing the rules of traffic in this particular situation.

When people object to Tillich's assertion that all knowledge of God is incurably symbolic and that symbols are the only language appropriate to religious faith, they are really objecting to the reduction of religious statements to signs. They are afraid that Tillich is turning Christian assertions about God into arbitrary designations which have no essential, intrinsic relation to the divine reality to which they point.

If symbols were no more than signs, there would, indeed, be no way of avoiding this kind of capricious subjectivism in theology. But this is not Tillich's position. As he has insisted again and again, all symbols, including religious symbols, participate in that to which they point. That is, they manifest and embody the reality which they symbolize without being identical with it; as a flag, for example, shares in the power and majesty of the nation which it symbolizes and is accorded the same respect as the nation itself. Because a symbol participates in the reality to which it points it is capable of opening up dimensions of that reality which would otherwise be closed to us. It is only when we are grasped by the power of some revelatory symbol that God's being is unveiled to us—whether that symbol is the word "Father," or "the Rock of Ages," or the bread and wine of the Communion meal, or Jesus as the Christ.

At the same time, as a religious symbol opens up to us hitherto unknown levels of the divine ground of our being, it also opens up to us unrealized and unplumbed depths of our own being. For example, the symbol of the cross has for centuries not only opened up for Christians an understanding of God's nature as love, but kindled in themselves potentialities for love which they could not otherwise have known or experienced.

With this positive appreciation of the unique power of religious symbols, we can anticipate some divergence in point of view between Tillich and Bultmann on the issue of demythologizing. For Tillich, myths, which are defined as "symbols of faith combined in stories about divine-human encounters," [5] are not dispensable in the way in which they are for Bultmann. Bultmann, it will be remembered, believes that it is possible to translate the myths of the New Testament without remainder into existential

[5] *Dynamics of Faith* (New York: Harper & Row, 1958), p. 49.

statements about the meaning of man's existence in relation to God. Once we have made this translation, then the myths can, at least in principle, be dispensed with, even though we may continue to find them useful in worship and popular communication. John Macquarrie's criticism of Bultmann's conception of the theological task epitomizes well the way in which Tillich provides the necessary corrective for Bultmann's one-sided approach: "Theology is concerned not only with statements about human existence but with statements about God and his activity as well—transcendent statements, if you like, which, because we lack categories for the understanding of transcendent being as such, can only be expressed in symbolic or mythical form." [6]

For Tillich, also, the myths of the Bible have ontological as well as existential significance. This follows from what we said of their twofold function in opening up for our understanding levels of both God's being and our own. Any language which is not symbolic or mythical in character is incapable of expressing and mediating either of these understandings. If demythologizing means looking for some nonmythical or nonsymbolic kind of language to communicate the insights of faith, Tillich is convinced it is an illegitimate enterprise.

While Tillich refuses to demythologize in Bultmann's sense, he does see the paramount necessity of deliteralizing the symbolic language of Scripture. This is simply to recognize a symbol as a symbol and a myth as a myth with the full consciousness that as finite entities they are incapable of literally representing the infinite, however much they

[6] John Macquarrie, *An Existentialist Theology* (London: SCM Press, 1955), p. 244.

may participate in and point to its power and meaning. A myth which is thus understood for what it is as a true pointer to an aspect of divine reality, but not a literal representation of it, is called by Tillich a "broken myth." The breaking of the myth does not entail, as in Bultmann's demythologizing, the finding of a substitute way of speaking so that the myth can be retired from use. It does, of course, require an interpretation of the content of the myth if it is to continue to speak with meaning and power.

This process of breaking the myths of the Bible often meets with violent and fanatical resistance on the part of those who see it as a threat to the security of their "unbroken mythological world." As Tillich sees it, there is a certain stage in the history of the race and the individual when literalism is legitimate—when, for example, children never think to question the literal truth of the mythical stories of the Bible. When, however, in the process of growing up, questions begin to intrude themselves as to the adequacy of a literal interpretation of these stories, the individual may move from this stage of natural literalism to what Tillich calls "reactive literalism." At this stage he resists the breaking of the myth by repressing, half-consciously, half-unconsciously, the questions which have arisen. This explains the fanaticism and tenacity with which the biblical literalist seeks to protect inviolate his unbroken world of myth.

This kind of reactive literalism must be rejected not only because it leads to destructive splitting of a man's personality and undermines his personal integrity but, even more important, because it is the very epitome of idolatry. This is a consideration of fundamental importance for the proper understanding of many aspects of Tillich's thought.

He has, in the name of what he calls "the Protestant principle," waged a running battle against every tendency to confuse any finite reality with the ultimate, whether that reality is a church or a book or a doctrine or a symbol of whatever kind. Literalism is just another form of idolatry which violates the Protestant principle and its insistence that God alone is entitled to unconditional reverence. "Literalism," says Tillich,

> deprives God of his ultimacy and, religiously speaking, of his majesty. It draws him down to the level of that which is not ultimate, the finite and conditional. . . . Faith, if it takes its symbols literally, becomes idolatrous! It calls something ultimate which is less than ultimate. Faith, conscious of the symbolic character of its symbols, gives God the honor which is due him.[7]

In my judgment, Tillich has rendered a real service to Protestants at this point. He has reminded us of the terrible danger of much "talking" about God, talking which often borders on profanity. We profane the mystery of God, we take his "name" in vain, whenever we glibly assume that our earthbound symbols are able to "wrap up" and possess the mystery of the Holy One. Too many sermons and public prayers convey the impression that, as far as our knowledge of God is concerned, we have it "all taped"; or, as Sir Leslie Stephen so pungently stated it, "We claim to know more about God than any entomologist would claim to know about the spots on the back of a beetle." [8] Such theological arrogance needs to be corrected by the reverent agnosticism which Tillich's view of theological

[7] *Dynamics of Faith*, p. 52.
[8] Pittenger, "Paul Tillich as a Theologian," p. 275.

language inspires. We need to remember that in the presence of God we are confronted by a meaningful mystery about which it is possible and appropriate for the Christian to speak with conviction but never with dogmatism. For through such symbols of the Christian revelation we are able at best, so the apostle reminds us, to "see through a glass darkly."

A literalistic interpretation of biblical symbols has led, Tillich believes, to an erroneous way of thinking and speaking of God which has put a false stumbling block in the way of modern man's acceptance of the Christian gospel. There are those who feel that his most important theological contribution is his emancipation of Christian thinking about God from the assumptions of a crude and naïve supranaturalism.[9] According to this view, God is represented as a being separate from other beings, occupying a supranatural realm above or beyond this world from which he descends to direct and control events in our world in accordance with his purposes.

On the basis of the flood of letters received during the *Honest to God* controversy, John A. T. Robinson is prepared to testify to the wide prevalence of such a view among church people today. His postbag confirms, he says, "that many popular religious ideas are still incredibly more naïve than bishops and clergy often suppose." [10] Moreover, his mail has served to strengthen his conviction that there are countless men and women both inside and

[9] Cf. Robinson, *Honest to God,* p. 56: "This, I believe, is Tillich's great contribution to theology—the reinterpretation of transcendence in a way which preserves its reality while detaching it from the projection of supranaturalism."

[10] *The Honest to God Debate,* p. 257.

outside the churches who are unable to think of God any longer in terms of the supranaturalistic scheme as existing "up there" or "out there." It is to this latter class of people that Tillich's interpretation of the nature of God comes with the force of an emancipation proclamation.

Tillich's view of God has been subject to frequent misunderstanding, not only because it goes against the grain of much popular piety which likes to think of God in cozy, personalistic terms, but because his own choice of technical language has often been more obscuring than clarifying. When he insists that faith must transcend the "God of theism" in order to apprehend the "God above God," [11] or when he asserts bluntly that "God does not exist," [12] it is not unnatural that the uninitiated might draw the conclusion that he is a pantheist or, even worse, an atheist.

What he means to convey, however, in such paradoxical assertions is not that God is not real and distinguishable from ourselves and our world; but that he is precisely that reality with which we are most intimately, profoundly, and, indeed, disturbingly confronted. He is not a being who resides somewhere "up in the blue," whose habitation Soviet cosmonauts might someday locate. He is the creative ground of everything that has being, without whose sustaining power nothing could exist. We meet him not in some extramundane spiritual retreat, but in the depths of our intramundane existence as life confronts us with the unconditional demands of truth and righteousness and love in our daily relationships and forces upon us questions of ultimate meaning and purpose. It is in the claim of the holy that emerges from the depths of life itself—

[11] *The Courage to Be* (New Haven: Yale University Press, 1952), ch. 6.
[12] *Systematic Theology,* I, 205.

from a civil rights struggle or the temptation of a shady business deal—that we are grasped and challenged by the divine holiness. It is in the experience of "the goodness of being" in our this-worldly encounters and relationships—in the joy of children's laughter or the selfless sacrifice of a friend—that we become aware of the grace that issues from the divine ground of our being and without which we could not live.

Tillich's interest in denying the existence of God as a superbeing is not to call into question his transcendent reality but, on the contrary, to safeguard it. The weakness of supranaturalism is that "it transforms the infinity of God into a finiteness which is merely an extension of the categories of finitude." [13] Thinking of God literally as a being alongside other beings, even if he is a supreme being, reduces him to the status of a finite reality subject to such categories as space, time, causality, and substance. Bringing God down to our level in this way not only robs him of the majesty and mystery of his divinity, but it makes it easier for us to evade the august demands of his holy presence:

In making God an object besides other objects, the existence and nature of which are matters of argument, theology supports the escape to atheism. It encourages those who are interested in denying the threatening Witness of their existence. The first step to atheism is always a theology which drags God down to the level of doubtful things. The game of the atheist is then very easy. For he is perfectly justified in destroying such a phantom and all its ghostly qualities. And because the theoretical atheist is just in his destruction, the practical

[13] *Systematic Theology,* II, 6.

atheists (all of us) are willing to use his argument to attempt to flee God.[14]

Tillich's concept of God as the ground of being has been criticized for being too emotionally neutral and impersonal to sustain a vital experience of prayer and worship. "Who would ever think of praying to the ground of being?" some have asked. The answer is, of course, no one, least of all Paul Tillich! The language of prayer and liturgy cannot dispense with personalistic images and symbols in addressing God if this language is to express the ultimate concern of personal beings. Tillich's view will permit us to continue to pray to God as Father. But when we do so we will be aware that we are speaking symbolically, and that personal terms like "Father," while expressing something profoundly true about God, point beyond themselves to an inexhaustible reality which defies literal description by finite minds.

Thus, while God is not a person in the sense in which we are persons, he is the ground of all that is personal. This means that he is not impersonal but suprapersonal. Tillich is convinced that with all its use of vivid personal imagery in describing God, the Bible "has the astonishing power to speak of the presence of the divine in such a way that the I-thou character of the relation never darkens the transpersonal power and mystery of the divine, and vice versa." [15] This is seen in Jesus' words about the Heavenly Father's numbering of the hairs of our heads and his noting of every sparrow's fall and in Paul's reference to

[14] *The Shaking of the Foundations,* pp. 45-46.

[15] *Biblical Religion and the Search for Ultimate Reality* (Chicago: University of Chicago Press, 1955), p. 84.

the way the Spirit assists us in our prayers "with sighs too deep for words." Such allusions as these suggest the participation of God in every event, human or natural, as the infinite power and ground by which it has its being.

Estrangement, Healing, and the New Being

God is not only the power of being. He is the power of "the New Being." He not only keeps everything that is from falling into nonbeing; he restores to man his essential being from which he has been alienated by sin, thereby creating in him "the courage to be" his true self. With this theme we are launched into a discussion of Tillich's doctrine of salvation, which is perhaps the central emphasis in his entire theology.

Tillich is very sensitive to the fact that the notion of salvation, particularly in many of its traditional formulations, is virtually meaningless to modern men. For this reason the roadside sign "Jesus saves" is less likely to be a meaningful communication than the occasion for jest and ridicule. In this situation the task of the theologian and the preacher is to reinterpret the meaning of salvation in such a way as to do justice both to the biblical symbols which describe it and the particular kinds of questions which men in our generation are raising about the meaning of their existence.

Tillich believes that a proper correlation of the questions of twentieth-century man with the biblical answers leads to an interpretation of salvation in terms of the idea of "healing." "In this sense, healing means reuniting that which is estranged, giving a center to what is split, overcoming the split between God and man, man and his world, man and himself."[16] Salvation as healing means the conquest of man's existential estrangement through the power of what Tillich calls the New Being. The result is the restoration of wholeness and health which entails, however fragmentarily, the attainment of man's essential being, the actualization of what God in creating him intended him to be.

Such a view of salvation presupposes an understanding of the human predicament as one of universal estrangement in which man is separated from God, from his fellowmen, and from himself. Tillich, in rejecting the literal historicity of the story of the fall and in interpreting it as a symbol of the transition from essence to existence, has left himself open to the charge that he had identified creation with the fall. Though his language in certain places might suggest such a conclusion, this is certainly not Tillich's intention. He is simply trying to make the point that wherever we come upon man or created existence we find estrangement. He is quite explicit that this state of estrangement is the consequence of both freedom and destiny. To the extent to which it is rooted in man's freedom, estrangement is sin.

Estrangement as sin has a threefold character. It is the willful turning away from the divine ground of our being (unbelief), combined with the elevation of our own selves to the center of all things, thus usurping the place of God (*hubris*). It expresses itself also in "concupiscence"—the lustful striving not only for sexual conquest, but for knowledge and power as well—in other words, "the un-

[16] *Systematic Theology,* II, 166.

limited desire to draw the whole of reality into one's self." [17]

This attempt on the part of man to draw everything into his own self as if it were the universal center results in the loss of both his self and his world. Man ceases to be a centered self in polar relationship with a structured world. He literally "falls to pieces" and, as as consequence, his world falls to pieces. The essential elements of his being are thrown into conflict with one another. His drive to assert his freedom ends up in an arbitrariness which forges the chains of his own bondage. His creative, self-transcending impulses struggle uneasily with the rigidities of a legalism which suppresses creative newness to static formalism. His effort to express his individuality is at war with his need to participate in community.

In the state of estrangement, the tension between these various polar elements of man's being, which is essential to his "health" as man, is broken, and as a result he is thrown into inner conflict. Not having a whole, integrated self he is unable to relate meaningfully to his world. And so he is driven into the despair of meaninglessness, a despair which is aggravated by the despair of guilt, for deep down he knows he is responsible for the estrangement in which he finds himself.

The question which this analysis of man's estranged existence raises for theology to answer, then, is the question of a power capable of healing these splits between man and his God, man and his world, and man and his own essential self. And the answer of Christian faith is that such a power is available—the power of a New Being

[17] *Ibid.*, p. 52.

which has appeared uniquely, though not exclusively, in Jesus as the Christ. The Christian evangel of salvation which Christ's disciples are called upon to address to those outside the circle of faith is this: "We want to communicate to you an experience we have had that here and there in the world and now and then in ourselves is a New Creation, usually hidden, but sometimes manifest, and certainly manifest in Jesus who is called the Christ." [18]

The Christian does not look, then, for his salvation to the power of an ideal which hovers ethereally above the actualities of historical existence. Tillich is not a gnostic or an idealist as some critics have tried to represent him. Whatever else is obscure in Tillich, this much at least is clear: that faith finds its ground of salvation in a concrete, historical person. This is the good news—that in this man Jesus of Nazareth, God, who is the ground of our being, manifests himself under the conditions of our estranged existence, conquering the destructive conflicts which have robbed us of the wholeness and health which God's creative purpose intended. Faith acclaims Jesus as the Christ because it has perceived in his deeds as well as in his death, in his words as well as in his deeds—in the totality of his personal life—the New Being which is none other than our own essential being. In this one who is "bone of our bone and flesh of our flesh," who endured all the handicaps of our human lot—its anxiety, its suffering, its homelessness, its temptations—we find nevertheless one in whom the marks of our sinful estrangement—unbelief, *hubris,* concupiscence—are totally absent. In his unique person the destructive split between God and man, man and his

[18] *The New Being,* p. 18.

neighbor, man and himself, is unambiguously overcome.

The uniqueness of Jesus as the Christ lies in the fact that here in his person is the only place in which the New Being is unambiguously and undistortedly actualized. This does not mean that the New Being is nowhere else evident, nor that salvation is exclusively restricted to that small percentage of men in history who by an arbitrary accident of birth have had the opportunity of an encounter with Jesus of Nazareth. Mankind is never left alone by God. The divine Spirit breaks through again and again into man's history in saving power.

There is a history of salvation (and revelation) which is wider than the history of God's mighty acts in and through Israel and the church. The New Being appears in other times and places than in that segment of time we call Christian history and those places where the church has extended its influence.

> It is present in a preparatory way, fragmentarily, and is open to demonic distortion. But it is present and heals where it is seriously accepted. On these healing forces the life of mankind always depends; they prevent the self-destructive structures of existence from plunging mankind into complete annihilation.[19]

While these healing structures are present here and there apart from their manifestation in Jesus as the Christ, he is the criterion by means of which we are able to discern them elsewhere, because only in him are they unambiguously expressed.

Tillich has used the concept of the "latent church" to

[19] *Systematic Theology,* II, 167.

give expression to this belief that the Spirit of God is creatively and redemptively at work in all history. The latent church, in contradistinction to the "manifest church," is to be found among those groups, both secular and religious, which exhibit something of the power of the New Being in their lives, even though not consciously exercising faith in Jesus as the Christ. Such groups may even show a greater sensitivity to human need and a more sincere openness to the claims of truth and justice than the churches themselves. When this happens, the latent church provides a much needed judgment upon the manifest church and a wholesome curb on ecclesiastical arrogance.

The latent church, however, lacks the ultimate criterion of the New Being as it has appeared in the Christ, and as a consequence it does not have a built-in corrective against demonic distortion as does the manifest church. However much the latter may fail to be open to the healing and renewing power of the New Being, as long as it is aware of its foundation in Jesus Christ, it at least knows better.

The Spiritual Community and the Churches

A number of years ago Theodore M. Greene wrote of Tillich: "His critique of historical Christianity would, if taken seriously, provoke revolutionary changes in the Church."[20] There is a good deal more supporting evidence for such a prophecy today, particularly since the appearance of Tillich's searching analysis of the nature and functions of the church in the recently published third volume of his *Systematic Theology*. His discussion of the way in

[20] Charles W. Kegley and Robert W. Bretall (eds.), *The Theology of Paul Tillich* (New York: The Macmillan Company, 1952), p. 50.

which the New Being becomes paradoxically actualized in the life of the churches is a rich mine of theological inspiration for Christian renewal and reform.

Tillich's understanding of the church is treated systematically in connection with that section of his work in which he correlates life and Spirit.[21] The church is for him the central, though not exclusive, manifestation of the victory of the divine Spirit over the ambiguities of life. The church really becomes the church when it is grasped by the power of the Spiritual Presence[22] and becomes thereby a Spiritual Community—a community of faith and love—in which the New Being is embodied.

Tillich's attitude toward the church is a blend of high expectations and sober realism. He is motivated by a deep faith that the healing and renewing power of the divine Spirit is effectively operative within the church in the creation of a Spiritual Community in which the estrangements and ambiguities of life are overcome. At the same time, he is realistically aware of the way in which the actual church on the corner so often miserably compromises the true meaning and reality of the church.

Full recognition of both the glory and ignominy of the church requires that we consistently view the relationship between the actual churches and the Spiritual Community in paradoxical terms: "The paradox of the churches is the fact that they participate, on the one hand, in the ambiguities of life in general and of the religious life in particular and, on the other hand, in the unambiguous life of the

[21] *Systematic Theology* (Chicago: The University of Chicago Press, 1963), Vol. III, Part IV.

[22] Tillich uses the symbol "Spiritual Presence" rather than "Spirit of God" in order to avoid the connotation of a separate being.

Spiritual Community."[23] The recognition of the various ramifications of this paradox is of vital importance in understanding the dynamics of apostasy and renewal in the life of the church.

The church shares in the ambiguities of all finite life which is alienated from its source and ground in God. In particular, it shares in the ambiguities of religion. These, as Tillich analyzes them, are two in number—the tendency of religion to become either profane or demonic.

The profanization of religion is its failure to point to the holy. The term "profane" literally means "remaining before the door of the temple" or "standing outside the holy." Thus profanization involves the acceptance of life in its finite dimensions only, while resisting the self-transcendence of the human spirit as it reaches out to the divine ground of its being.

On the level of organized religion as well as individual religious experience, profane elements inevitably creep in.

> Instead of transcending the finite in the direction of the infinite, institutionalized religion actually becomes a finite reality itself—a set of prescribed activities to be performed, a set of stated doctrines to be accepted, a social pressure group along with others, a political power with all the implications of power politics.[24]

It is the distortion of the church's life by the profane which justifies many common criticisms of the institutional church—its superficiality and pettiness, the mechanization and routinization of its life, the exaltation of ecclesiastical organization and churchly activities as ends in themselves,

[23] *Systematic Theology,* III, 165.
[24] *Ibid.,* p. 99.

the reduction of religion to a dull habit and a meaningless ritual. While the church must everlastingly fight against surrender to these profane forces in its life, Tillich cautions against the "utopian fallacy" implicit in much of the current clamor against the institutional church which assumes that it is possible to eliminate completely the element of the profane. This is to overlook the inescapable ambiguity of life which the church as a sociological community cannot avoid. There is no way in which the holy can be received in history except through profanized religious forms which to some extent resist it. We must learn to listen for the "still small voice of the Spirit" above "the noise of solemn assemblies."

There is a further ambiguity of religion to which the church is subject. This is the ambiguity introduced by the element of the demonic. "The demonic does not resist self-transcendence as does the profane, but it distorts self-transcendence by identifying a particular bearer of holiness with the holy itself." [25] The demonic always involves the claim of a finite reality to infinite power and significance.

The inevitable result of demonization is the splitting of either a community or an individual personality. A nation is thrown into conflict with its neighbors when it makes demonic claims of absoluteness for its system of values. Analogously, when a particular set of forces in the personality are accorded absolute superiority while other forces are suppressed, the result is a split personality. The fruits of the demonic are always personal and cultural disintegration.

The force of the demonic is intensified in the realm of

[25] *Ibid.*, p. 102.

religion because of the ease with which the religious forms which are bearers of the holy can be confused with the holy itself. The fanaticism and fury with which religiously consecrated groups, customs, doctrines, or ideals are defended against criticism is a measure of their demonic distortion. The life of the churches provides ample documentation of such distortion. The demonic is to be found, for example, in the attempt, in the name of the holy, to defend a racially segregated pattern of church life against every appeal of love and justice; it is to be found in the suppression of honest obedience to the demands of truth in the interests of preserving inviolate a sacred set of dogmas; it is to be found in the stunting of a person's full humanity by a puritanical ideal of asceticism which is sanctioned by a compulsive religious quest for personal holiness.

While the churches as sociological communities are inextricably enmeshed in the ambiguities of profanization and demonization which have just been described, this is only one side of the paradox which defines their nature. For every church has a theological as well as a sociological character. This duality is Tillich's substitute for the traditional Reformation distinction between the visible and invisible church. It has the advantage, he believes, of avoiding the impression made by the older distinction that the true church is some kind of entity beside or behind the visible, historical church—a conception which subtly downgrades the latter.

There is but one church, Tillich says, and this one church has both sociological and theological aspects. Its theological character is its existence as a Spiritual Community which participates in the unambiguous life of the Spirit. The Spiritual Community is, as it were, the inner goal and essence of the churches, that which is the source of everything which makes them churches and not just social clubs. It is not an ideal which hovers behind the reality of the churches, but an effective power for their renewal (the power of the New Being) which struggles constantly against their ambiguities.

Concretely, the Spiritual Community manifests itself in the churches in the creation of actual communities of faith and love. This does not mean that the ambiguities of religion are thereby eliminated. But they are conquered in principle and their destructive and disintegrating force is broken. That is to say, by being recognized and resisted as violations of the Christian norm, the power of the profane and demonic is undermined, if not completely removed.

This occurs, first of all, to the extent to which the churches become genuine communities of faith. The faith which is a mark of the Spiritual Community must be distinguished, however, from the distortions of faith which have appeared so frequently in the history of the church. Faith has been erroneously identified with one or other of the psychological functions—intellect, will, or feeling. True faith, which is a centered act of a whole self caught up in an ultimate concern, must be rescued from such false notions.[26] Faith is not believing something that has a low degree of evidence (the intellectualistic distortion of faith); it is not cajoling the will into submission to an arbitrary authority (the voluntaristic distortion of faith); it is not wallowing in vague, subjective emotions (the emotionalistic distortion of faith). All these distortions of faith lead to demonic by-products in the life of the church, and

[26] See *Dynamics of Faith,* ch. 2.

their presence is a reminder of the fragmentary and incomplete conquest of the ambiguities of life by the Spiritual Presence.

While all of man's psychical powers—mental, volitional, and emotional—participate in the act of faith, it is the divine Spirit rather than any functions of the human psyche which produces faith. The faith which brings the Spiritual Community to birth is "the state of being grasped by the Spiritual Presence and opened to the transcendent unity of unambiguous life"; or, in a christological frame of reference, it is "the state of being grasped by the New Being as it is manifest in Jesus as the Christ." [27]

The fact that faith involves an immediate awareness of being grasped by the divine Spirit means that it includes at its heart an element of certainty. This certainty of the Spiritual Presence does not, however, eradicate the possibility of doubt, as much popular piety has assumed. Far from regarding doubt as sin (that is, if it is honest existential doubt), Tillich regards it as an integral element in the structure of faith. The presence of doubt in faith is, in fact, testimony to the seriousness of faith as the expression of an ultimate concern. There is no genuine faith without an "in spite of" element which is overcome by a venture of courageous affirmation.

In the light of Tillich's analysis, much so-called faith in the churches is rendered suspect by virtue of a blandness and escapism which has never really confronted the risk involved in faith. Such counterfeit faith is blind to both the terror and the glory of life because it lacks the courage to plumb life to its depths. Its placidity is the mark of its essential "profanity."

[27] *Systematic Theology,* III, 131.

Churches which try to repress the element of doubt in faith are dangerously vulnerable to demonic error. The Roman Catholic Church has made itself particularly susceptible to this error by claiming divine authority for its own doctrinal formulations. The Protestant principle rejects all such attempts to foreclose the possibility of doubt with respect to any dogmatic interpretations of the faith. This means that membership in the community of faith does not call for the demonic act of "unconditional subjection to the doctrinal statements of faith as they have developed in the rather ambiguous history of the churches." [28] It requires only the daring affirmation that Jesus is the Christ, the bringer of the New Being. He who affirms this is included in the community of faith; he who denies it automatically excludes himself.

If the church as the Spiritual Community receives the New Being in faith, it actualizes it concretely through love. The church as a community of love presupposes a relationship between members which "expresses itself in mutual acceptance in spite of the separations which take place because the church is a sociologically determined group." [29] This means that the cohesive which holds the church together is not manufactured out of the natural preferences of people which are rooted in social, economic, educational, racial, or temperamental compatibilities. The "glue" which unites people of varying backgrounds and dispositions into a Spiritual Community is the reconciling love of the cross which unconditionally affirms the other person in terms of his essential humanity. The reuniting

[28] *Ibid.*, p. 174.
[29] *Ibid.*, p. 178.

power of *agape,* not the chumminess of social affinity, is the basis for a true Spiritual Community.

A genuine community of love must continuously exercise a prophetic judgment against everything which negates love. It judges both those within the community and those outside it. With respect to the internal discipline of the church, Tillich sees a real weakness in lay-dominated Protestantism. In many churches the minister is bereft of the authority to represent the community of love against the distortions brought into the church's life by the sociological involvements and secular loyalties of its members. The consequences can be disastrous:

> This makes a prophetic judgment of the congregations, including their most powerful sociological groups, so difficult as to be almost impossible. The result is often the sociologically determined, class church so conspicuous in American Protestantism. In the name of a tactful and cautious approach (which in itself is desirable), the judging function of the community of love is suppressed. This situation probably hurts the church more than an open attack on its principles launched by deviating and erring members.[30]

Tillich sees three ways in which the church as a community of love relates itself to the society around it. Each of these ways is analogous to one of the three christological affirmations which describe Christ as priest, prophet, and king:

1. The first is the way of "silent interpenetration." Through quiet influence and indirect education there is a "continuous radiation of the Spiritual essence of the

[30] *Ibid.,* p. 180.

churches into all groups of the society in which they live" and a "pouring of priestly substance into the social structure of which the churches are a part." [31]

2. The second is the prophetic way of "critical judgment." This is the open attack on the negativities of a particular society in the name of the Spiritual Presence. Tillich also commends "a kind of reverse prophetism" according to which the tables are turned and the church becomes the object of prophetic criticism from the world. This is made possible on his assumption that a latent Spiritual Community exists outside the churches. Thus the Spirit is free to use secular movements such as organized labor, civil rights groups, the Supreme Court—even communism—to prod the church into a revision of its interpretations of justice and humanity.

3. Finally, there is the way of "political establishment." Just as the Crucified Christ had a royal office, so the church must humbly exercise a political office, using the tools of political influence to extend the sway of the Spiritual Presence in society.

Recognizing the ambiguity of all political means, Protestant churches have usually had an uneasy conscience when they have entered the political area. Their caution is justified insofar as involvement in political activity may become the expression of a "pseudo-Spiritual will to power"—a species of demonic *hubris*—more than a sincere effort to transform the structures of society according to the norm of the New Being. This danger, however, does not make it any less necessary for the church to use political instruments to fight against those social forces which negate love

[31] *Ibid.*, p. 213.

and justice. The priestly and prophetic impact of the church on the social order must be reinforced by carefully selected political weapons which are consistent with the character of the church as a Spiritual Community.

The Protestant Principle: The Keystone of the Arch

It has been possible in this brief survey to describe only a small number of the materials which have gone into Tillich's monumental bridge-building enterprise. The experts will continue to debate about the soundness of the structure which has taken shape as Tillich has thrown his massive theological span over the various boundary lines which separate the answers of the Christian revelation from the questions of modern man. It is hardly necessary, however, to await the outcome of these technical evaluations in order to recognize and put to use the prophetic impetus for renewal inherent in many of Tillich's conceptions.

The prophetic spirit which breathes through all Tillich's writing is perhaps best explained by a key principle which is never far from the surface of any discussion in which he engages. This is what he calls the Protestant principle. More than any other single conception it gives unity and coherence to everything he says. It may, indeed, be regarded as the keystone which holds together Tillich's theological arch[32]—an arch which, as we have seen, is grounded on the one side in the biblical revelation and on the other in the contemporary human situation. The

[32] The figure of the arch has been used recently in a somewhat different context by Barth's successor, Heinrich Ott, to illuminate the nature of the theological enterprise. Cf. his discussion of the "hermeneutical arch" in James M. Robinson and John B. Cobb, Jr. (eds.), *The Later Heidegger and Theology* (New York: Harper & Row, 1963), pp. 78-82.

Protestant principle provides the clue to the way in which these polarities are kept together in constructive tension.

Tillich summarizes the meaning of this key concept as follows:

> The Protestant principle . . . contains the divine and human protest against any absolute claim made for a relative reality, even if this claim is made by a Protestant church. . . . It is the guardian against the attempts of the finite and conditioned to usurp the place of the unconditional in thinking and acting. It is the prophetic judgment against religious pride, ecclesiastical arrogance, and secular self-sufficiency and their destructive consequences.[33]

Tillich sees the Protestant principle as the theological expression of the true relationship between God and man. It is rooted in the Reformers' doctrine of justification by grace through faith alone. When men come to realize that their acceptance by God is not based on any possession of unambiguous righteousness or truth but solely upon divine grace, they are no longer under the compulsion to deceive themselves about themselves. This recognition breaks the back of all self-justifying, idolatrous claims. It leaves open the door for a principle of self-criticism—the Protestant principle—which acknowledges the superiority of God over all his manifestations in finite, human experience.

It is not difficult to detect the mark of the Protestant principle on all Tillich's theological ideas. It is seen in the method of correlation which protects the theologian from the arrogance of slick solutions which are not wrested from his own conscious identification with the questions and

[33] *The Protestant Era* (Chicago: University of Chicago Press, 1948), p. 163.

ambiguities of the human predicament. It is reflected in his insistence upon the symbolic character of all our knowledge of God and his battle against all literalizing and supranaturalizing tendencies which bring God down to our level and confuse our finite categories with the infinite. It is evident in his affirmation of man's universal estrangement from his true being and the real but fragmentary restoration of that being through acceptance of Jesus as the Christ. Above all, it is determinative in his understanding of the church. The churches can be called holy not because of their actual holiness, but because they have the principle of reformation within themselves in the power of the Spiritual Community to judge and transform.

Tillich recognized that the Protestant principle by itself was not enough. It needed to be balanced by what he called the "Catholic substance," that is, the sacramental and mystical emphasis on the concrete embodiment of the Spiritual Presence. We need the criticism by the Protestant principle of every human claim to unconditional truth and holiness. But we need also the confidence, which Protestantism sometimes lacks, that the Spiritual Presence *does* become manifest in concrete realities of space and time; that the New Being *does,* from time to time, take on flesh and blood in individuals and communities; and that the Spiritual Community *does* become a reality in the churches despite the ambiguity of their institutions and traditions. It is in the maintenance of this paradoxical tension between the Protestant principle and the Catholic substance that the continued renewal of the church is assured. In their union is the promise of those shaking and transforming experiences of *kairos* when God breaks into our history in judgment and in healing.

V

REINHOLD NIEBUHR
THE IMPLICATIONS OF CHRISTIAN REALISM

The earliest published book about Reinhold Niebuhr reflects an assessment of the prophetic significance of his thought in the very title: *Reinhold Niebuhr: Prophet from America.* The concluding judgment of its English author might be regarded as a vindication, if such were needed, of our inclusion of Niebuhr in this study of the most influential prophetic voices of the theology of our era:

Reinhold Niebuhr is a gift of God to a tortured and troubled world. He is, by any standard of judgment whatsoever, a leading, if not the leading theorist in the contemporary revolution in Christian thought. He has made orthodox theology relevant to our secular crisis. . . . By his prophetic insight and passion, he has made the Christian faith an inescapable issue for a generation whose own secular faith has proved to be bankrupt. This achievement makes his place secure in the apostolic succession of Christian revolutionaries.[1]

As we have seen, it was the prophetic voice of Karl Barth which precipitated a full-scale theological revolution on

[1] David R. Davies, *Reinhold Niebuhr: Prophet from America* (New York: The Macmillan Company, 1948), pp. 101-2.

the Continent in the early 1920's. It fell to the lot of Reinhold Niebuhr to do much the same thing for American theology about a decade later. Niebuhr's theology provided a more congenial bridge from liberalism to neo-orthodoxy for most American thinkers than did the early Barth. No doubt one of the reasons for this was the apologetic concern which consistently dominated his thought from the beginning. Much of the prophetic impact of his work has stemmed from his remarkable success in demonstrating the relevance of biblical faith for the complex problems of our modern secular world. Unlike Barth, he has conceived it to be his business as a theologian to enter into debate with secular alternatives to the Christian faith with a view to showing that, in the final analysis, only a Christian understanding of human nature and destiny is capable of doing full justice to the heights and the depths of man's personal and social existence. Thus it is his job to turn men from false hopes of redemption and finally induce the confession: "Lord to whom shall we go? Thou hast the words of eternal life."

Niebuhr has always been impatient with what he feels is a failure in Barth's theology to illumine "the foothills where human life must be lived." The magnificent testimony of this theology to the ultimate triumph of divine grace over human sin can inspire men to heroic action in times of great historical crisis such as occurred with the rise of Hitler's demonism. But it is much less successful in providing concrete guidance for the day-to-day decisions which men must make in the morally ambiguous situations which confront them as politicians, businessmen, or citizens. The Barthian theology, Niebuhr believes, can too readily degenerate into a form of social irresponsibility "when the divine grace is regarded as a way of escape from, rather than a source of engagement with, the anxieties, perplexities, sins, and pretensions of human existence." [2]

It has been Niebuhr's lifelong persistence in entering into costly engagement, on both theoretical and practical levels, with the concrete problems which men face in the social order that has given his theological ideas the relevance and prophetic power which they undoubtedly possess. His theology has been wrought out step by step in conjunction with his attempt to act responsibly as a Christian in relation to the pressing problems of social, economic, and political life. The result has been the production of a brand of down-to-earth Christian realism, delivered from the naïveté of much idealistic and orthodox Christianity, which brings the gospel into saving contact with the tragic conflicts and confusions of real life.

The Making of a Christian Realist

To appreciate fully the peculiar genius of Niebuhr's theology of Christian realism, it is necessary to see how it grew out of the involvements and tensions of his own eventful life. He was born in a midwest manse, the son of a German Evangelical pastor in Wright City, Missouri. His father was a man of rather liberal leanings who early introduced him to the writings of the German theologian Harnack. After graduating from his denominational college and seminary, he went to Yale with the intention of preparing himself for a career in teaching. It was not long, however, before he became bored with his theological studies,

[2] D. B. Robertson (ed.), *Essays in Applied Christianity* (New York: Meridian Books, 1959), p. 174.

which seemed increasingly irrelevant to the real world around him. Satisfying himself with an M.A. degree, he took a small struggling pastorate in Detroit.

During the thirteen years he served the church its membership increased from 40 to some 800 members. This demonstration of his effectiveness as a builder of churches was by no means, however, the most significant development of those thirteen years. Far more important for the years to come was the painful process of theological reconstruction which these Detroit years forced upon him.

These were the years when Henry Ford was beginning to build his vast automobile empire. Niebuhr's firsthand observations of the bruising impact of the harsh realities of modern industrialism on the lives of men and women in his own parish did more than the reading of books to reshape his theological outlook in a more realistic direction. Up until this time Niebuhr had rather uncritically adhered to the highly optimistic and moralistic creed of theological liberalism which was the fashion of the day. What Henry Ford was doing to members of his flock forced him, however, to revise the optimistic assumptions about human nature which were so much a part of his inherited liberal faith. His sensitive spirit recoiled against the brutality of the Ford industrial organization, which amassed huge profits at the expense of untold suffering perpetrated upon the workers in the days prior to the organization of labor. Niebuhr was particularly irritated by the moral pretensions of Henry Ford, who attempted to build a reputation for benevolence through his much advertised five-day-a-week and five-dollars-a-day policies. He was close enough to the plight of individual workers to know that these pretensions of generosity masked conditions of acute human suffering brought on by such things as work speed-ups, uncompensated layoffs for long periods of retooling, and the depersonalizing slavery of assembly-line technology.

Niebuhr's lifelong passion for social justice was kindled in this furnace of personal involvement in the hurts and sufferings of the victims of economic exploitation. It was inevitable that these experiences should do something to his theology. They provided for him a liberal education in the subtlety with which a high-sounding idealism can be corrupted by self-interest, the hypocrisy and self-deception which men resort to in their desperate efforts to conceal their self-interest, and the destructive consequences which result when men's will to power is allowed to assert itself unchecked. Further, it convinced him of the impotence of the moralistic approach of idealism to problems of social and economic justice. He soon saw the futility of trying to move men like Henry Ford by moral preachments and appeals to "Christian idealism." He was later to elaborate theologically the insight forged out of the crucible of his Detroit experience: that Christian love can be made relevant to life in an industrial society only when it takes the form of a realistic grappling with the harsh facts of collective power and injustice.

Niebuhr became increasingly appalled at the failure of the church and its ministry to utter a relevant and prophetic word in the midst of the revolutionary changes going on all around them. A revealing diary which he kept during those years, later published under the title *Leaves from the Notebooks of a Tamed Cynic,* is full of barbed criticisms of the church's irrelevance which have not lost their point in the intervening years. Following an eye-opening tour of one of the big automobile factories he wrote this:

Beside the brutal facts of modern industrial life, how futile are our homiletical spoutings! The church is undoubtedly cultivating graces and preserving spiritual amenities in the more protected area of society. But it isn't challenging the essential facts of modern industrial civilization by a hair's breadth. It isn't even thinking about them.[3]

Much of the church's lack of prophetic relevance Niebuhr puts down to the minister's habit of keeping his utterances safely on the level of pious generalities:

One of the most fruitful sources of self-deception in the ministry is the proclamation of great ideals and principles without any clue to their relation to the controversial issues of the day. The minister feels very heroic in uttering the ideals because he knows that some rather dangerous immediate consequences are involved in their application. But he doesn't make the application clear, and those who hear his words are either unable to see the immediate issue involved or they are unconsciously grateful to the preacher for not belaboring a contemporaneous issue which they know to be involved.[4]

That is every bit as true, Niebuhr would say, today in the midst of the racial revolution of the 60's as it was during the economic revolution of the 20's. Nobody can be a prophet in any age without being embarrassingly specific.

Niebuhr was devastatingly caustic in his criticism of ministers who are so dependent on the largess of their con-

[3] *Leaves from the Notebooks of a Tamed Cynic* (New York: Meridian Books, 1957), p. 100.

[4] *Ibid.*, pp. 218-19.

gregations that they sacrifice the integrity of honest speaking from the pulpit. After being driven home one day by a ministerial colleague in a big Packard car which was the gift of his congregation, Niebuhr made this entry in his diary: "ministers who can preach the gospel of Jesus in our kind of civilization without making anyone uncomfortable deserve an automobile for the difficult feat. And they need one to compensate them for that lack of spiritual vitality which makes the performance of the feat possible."[5] Niebuhr goes on to add with characteristic candor: "But all this may be the voice of jealousy. I love nothing so much in the realm of physical pleasures as the sense of power which comes from 'stepping on the gas' when ensconsed in a big car."

Niebuhr was long enough in the active pastorate to learn to appreciate the difficulty of maintaining a genuinely prophetic ministry in the local church. It is not always simply a matter of cowardice or servile economic dependence. "I think the real clue to the tameness of a preacher," Niebuhr wrote, "is the difficulty one finds in telling unpleasant truths to people whom one has learned to love." It is not easy to speak the truth unqualifiedly when the objects of your strictures are people with whom you have established personal attachments. "I'm not surprised," Niebuhr observed, "that most budding prophets are tamed in time to become harmless parish priests." [6]

Only when the minister avoids the self-righteous assumption that he himself has arrived can he presume to don the prophet's mantle. The *Leaves* are replete with indications that Niebuhr was realistically aware of his own limita-

[5] *Ibid.,* p. 213.
[6] *Ibid.,* p. 74.

tions and mixed motives. He was as merciless in exposing cowardice, temporizing, and excessive caution when he discovered it in himself as when he saw it in others. He was as sensitive to the danger of self-deception and humbug in himself as in others. And he was as conscious of the perils of egoistic exploitation and sinful will to power in the ministry as he was of its more blatant manifestations in the captains of industry. This refreshing realism about the complexity and corruptibility of his own motives as well as those of others was indispensable equipment for the prophetic office which Niebuhr was to exercise so powerfully throughout his career.

Niebuhr's training in the school of Christian realism continued in the academic environment of Union Theological Seminary, New York, where he was called in 1928 to become a professor of Christian Ethics. On first arriving at Union, he was acutely aware of his scholarly inadequacy, and he confessed later that it was "a full decade before I could stand before a class and answer the searching questions of the students at the end of a lecture without the sense of being a fraud who pretended to a larger and more comprehensive knowledge than I possessed." [7] The pressure of academic discipline soon began to take care of whatever gaps there may have been in Niebuhr's knowledge. An increased exposure to systematic biblical studies as well as the theological classics, particularly Augustine, completed his emancipation from the presuppositions of idealistic liberalism. By 1939 his theological position had matured to the point where he was invited to give the

[7] Charles W. Kegley and Robert W. Bretall (eds.), *Reinhold Niebuhr: His Religious, Social, and Political Thought* (New York: The Macmillan Company, 1956), pp. 8-9.

famous Gifford Lectures at the University of Edinburgh on "The Nature and Destiny of Man."

These lectures, along with numerous other books and articles, represent the fruitage not only of disciplined scholarship but turbulent participation in the world of public affairs. Becoming a seminary professor did not mean for Niebuhr a retreat to a sheltered academic cloister. His boundless energy was channeled into a host of activities through which he sought to apply his theological insights to concrete problems of social, economic, and political life. While he was still a pacifist (a position which he later abandoned) he was chairman of the leading American pacifist organization, the Fellowship of Reconciliation. He was one of the founders of the Fellowship of Socialist Christians, and more recently a leader of the New York Liberal party and the Americans for Democratic Action. After an earlier flirtation with Marxist ideas, he became one of the most trenchant critics of the utopian illusions and self-righteous idolatry of the communist ideology.

The results of this continual commerce between Niebuhr's theological insights and his firsthand confrontation with the real problems of the everyday world are best seen in the flood of articles which he produced for secular and religious journals.[8] In these provocative analyses of current affairs, the implications of his Christian realism for a wide variety of issues has been set forth. Here theology takes on flesh and blood and provides an illuminating perspective for reading "the signs of the times."

[8] Niebuhr has had a hand in editing two journals—*Radical Religion*, begun in 1935 and changing its name to *Christianity and Society* in 1940, and merging in 1956 with *Christianity and Crisis*, to which Niebuhr still contributes editorial leadership and comment.

Often Niebuhr's analyses are very subtle—exasperatingly so for those who want simple, straightforward solutions to every problem. This quality of his thought is the consequence of a realism which insists on facing the facts head on in all their incongruity and complexity. Such humility before the facts makes his thought incurably dialectical; that is, with every Yes there is always the qualifying No. Niebuhr is as impatient with the oversimplifications of the revivalist preacher as he is with the rationalist philosopher who tries to bend the facts to fit the procrustean bed of some premature scheme of rational coherence. There is, he feels, an ineradicable element of incoherence in the biblical faith. This is why it is capable of illuminating such mysteries as selfhood, sin, and grace—realities which cannot be caught up in any neat explanatory formulas. In dealing with historical reality, complicated as it is by freedom and sin, the tension of an unresolved paradox may be a more honest way to read the facts than a logically tidy but oversimplified explanation.[9]

The dialectical balance of Niebuhr's realism is admirably illustrated in a passage in which he critically appropriates the fruits of Reformation thought. This statement, incidentally, constitutes one of the best summaries of the significance of his life's work to be found anywhere in his writings:

> Reformation insights must be related to the whole range of human experience more "dialectically" than the Reformation succeeded in doing. The "yes" and "no" of its dialectical

[9] Cf. Niebuhr's essay on "Coherence, Incoherence, and Christian Faith" in *Christian Realism and Political Problems* (New York: Charles Scribner's Sons, 1953).

affirmations: that the Christian is *"justus et peccator,"* "both sinner and righteous"; that history fulfills and negates the Kingdom of God; that grace is continuous with, and in contradiction to, nature; that Christ is what we ought to be and also what we cannot be; that the power of God is in us and that the power of God is against us in judgment and mercy; that all these affirmations which are but varied forms of the one central paradox of the relation of the Gospel to history must be applied to the experiences of life from top to bottom. There is no area of life where "grace" does not impinge. There are no complex relations of social justice to which the love of the Kingdom of God is not relevant. There are on the other hand no areas or experiences where historical insecurity and anxiety are completely transcended, except in principle. There are indeed moments of prayer and, perhaps, ecstatic achievements of *agape* in which men are caught up in the "seventh heaven"; but these moments are merely an "earnest" of the fulfillment of life and must not be claimed as a possession. There is, finally, the transcendence of man over history and sin by faith. But that is also an "earnest"; and is corrupted like the manna in the wilderness when stored up as a secure possession.[10]

The Roots of Christian Realism: The Doctrine of Man

"One of the great misinterpretations of Niebuhr," John C. Bennett has written, "is the idea that he is the great pessimist of modern theology." [11] Following a Niebuhr lecture in Swanwick, England, the then Archbishop of Canterbury,

[10] *The Nature and Destiny of Man* (New York: Charles Scribner's Sons, 1943), II, 204.

[11] "Reinhold Niebuhr's Social Ethics" in *Reinhold Niebuhr: Religious, Social, Political Thought,* p. 49.

William Temple, composed a limerick which epitomized this misunderstanding in a lighthearted vein:

> At Swanwick, when Niebuhr had quit it,
> Said a young man: "At last I have hit it.
> Since I cannot do right,
> I must find out tonight
> The best sin to commit—and commit it.[12]

Niebuhr has pleaded guilty to this kind of charge by acknowledging that it was a long time before he "paid as much attention to the Christian conception of the cure as to the diagnosis, to grace as well as to sin." [13] Quite apart from that mistake, however, he is convinced, and no doubt rightly so, that any challenge by Christian realism of the utopian optimism and sentimental illusions of modern thought, in both its secular and religious varieties, would have been regarded as fundamentally pessimistic. It was inevitable that Niebuhr's sustained and skillful attack on the prevailing cultural and religious optimism of his day would earn him the reputation of being a pessimist, if not an outright cynic.

The truth of the matter is, however, that Niebuhr is far from being either. Cynicism, as he sees it, is the fate of the disappointed idealist. It is the product of the disillusionment which sets in when experience fails to bear out the naïve expectations of an uncritical optimism. The genius of biblical realism is its ability to see clearly the indeterminate possibilities for both good and evil in human

[12] June Bingham, *Courage to Change: An Introduction to the Life and Thought of Reinhold Niebuhr* (New York: Charles Scribner's Sons, 1961), p. 140.

[13] *Niebuhr: Religious, Social, Political Thought,* p. 10.

nature and history so that it is able to escape the pitfalls inherent in the extremes of cynicism and optimism. Niebuhr has been remarkably successful in elaborating the implications of this realism of biblical faith in a view of man which is as free from utopian illusions about human progress as it is from pessimistic defeatism. No statement from his writings expresses so well the delicate balance between optimism and pessimism which he has sought to maintain than his famous epigram about democracy: "Man's capacity for justice makes democracy possible; but man's inclination to injustice makes democracy necessary." [14]

The roots of Niebuhr's Christian realism are to be found in his penetrating analysis of the origin and nature of sin. He has done more than any other living theologian to document from empirical observations and introspective analysis the subtlety and intractability of sin at all levels of personal and social life. Only the Christian faith is able to take the full measure of the evil in man because it alone sees that its locus is at the very center of the self and that it is inextricably bound up with the same unique capacities of freedom which are the source of man's dignity and nobility. "The Christian estimate of human evil is so serious precisely because it places evil at the very centre of human personality: in the will." [15]

Idealistic and rationalistic views of human nature, both ancient and modern, make the mistake of locating man's problem somewhere outside his essential self, in the

[14] *The Children of Light and the Children of Darkness* (New York: Charles Scribner's Sons, 1944), p. xi.

[15] *The Nature and Destiny of Man* (New York: Charles Scribner's Sons, 1941), I, 16.

"drag" of his natural impulses or the imperfections of his institutions. This way of looking at man leads to the complacency of an easy conscience and the unwarranted optimism of the modern idea of progress. It places inordinate confidence in the possibility of a perfect society achieved by extending the control of man's rational faculties over ever wider areas of his life. Such utopianism overlooks the fact that even man's rationality and spirituality have been poisoned by sin, and that therefore every new creative achievement of the human spirit contains within it the seeds of further disharmony and destructiveness. "The conclusion most abhorrent to the modern mood," Niebuhr writes, "is that the possibilities of evil grow with the possibilities of good, and that human history is therefore not so much a chronicle of the progressive victory of the good over evil, of cosmos over chaos, as the story of an ever-increasing cosmos, creating ever-increasing possibilities of chaos." [16]

The problem of sin arises out of man's ambiguous situation as both finite and free, as a being who stands at the juncture of nature and spirit. On the one hand, he is a child of nature, sharing in the dependence, finitude, limitations, and mortality of all creaturely reality. On the other hand, he is a free spirit possessed with an infinite power of transcending himself and his world. This capacity for self-transcendence, which expresses itself in man's amazing gifts of memory and imagination, and his ability to stand outside himself and judge his own actions in the light of a self-chosen total end are the source of his dignity as a creature made in the image of God. This explains the restless-

[16] *An Interpretation of Christian Ethics* (London: SCM Press, 1936), p. 108.

ness of the human spirit, which by reason of its infinite power of self-transcendence can find its home only in the infinity of God.

Man's radical freedom to transcend the limitations of nature and self is, however, not only the secret of man's grandeur but the source of his misery as well. As a paradoxical mixture of finiteness and freedom, man is basically anxious. His anxiety, as such, is not sin, for it is the basis of all human creativity. Not knowing the limits of his possibilities he is goaded on in a ceaseless effort to transcend his present imperfections and limitations, attempting ever new conquests in the world of space as well as in the realm of the spirit. Though anxiety is therefore not sin, it is the spiritual state which inevitably tempts man to sin; it is what Niebuhr calls "the internal precondition of sin."[17]

Sin, in its essence, is man's vain attempt to overcome the insecurity of his ambiguous position as both finite and free. At bottom, it is his unbelieving refusal to accept the position assigned to him by his Creator. This rebellion against God expresses itself in two different ways which are, in effect, two different strategies by means of which the self tries frantically to allay the intolerable anxiety of its existence. On the one hand, man seeks to deny his creaturely limitations, makes himself the absolute center of his universe, and, in so doing, usurps the place of God. On the other hand, he may attempt to escape his God-given vocation of freedom and its attendant anxieties by surrendering to the impulses of nature. Thus, the idolatry of pride and the escapism of sensuality are the characteristic forms of man's sin:

[17] *The Nature and Destiny of Man,* I, 182.

When anxiety has conceived it brings forth both pride and sensuality. Man falls into pride when he seeks to raise his contingent existence to unconditional significance; he falls into sensuality when he seeks to escape from his unlimited possibilities of freedom, from the perils and responsibilities of self-determination, by immersing himself into a "mutable good," by losing himself in some natural vitality.[18]

Of these two forms of sin, Niebuhr says, pride is the more basic. This is attested by the fact that many instances of sensual indulgence—for example, luxurious living, drunkenness, or sexual conquest—are as much attempts to enhance the prestige of the ego as to find an anodyne to escape from the tensions of life. In any case, sensuality is not sinful because it involves the gratification of the desires of the body. Only as it becomes a distorted expression of a man's spirituality is it sinful; that is to say, only when it becomes a vehicle of man's inordinate self-love and an instrument of his self-aggrandizement.

Niebuhr would reverse the emphasis in much historic as well as contemporary Christianity which deals more harshly with the sins of the flesh than with the spiritual sin of pride. In making pride the basic sin, Niebuhr has drawn the criticism that his categories "fail adequately to account for the sins of the weak man as they do so forcefully for those of the strong man." [19] It might be questioned whether this is a matter of adequate categories or relative emphasis. Undoubtedly, Niebuhr gives the bulk of his attention to the sins of the strong man. But he does so because he has seen that their objective consequences in our modern tech-

[18] *Ibid.*, p. 186.

[19] William J. Wolf, "Reinhold Niebuhr's Doctrine of Man" in *Reinhold Niebuhr: Religious, Social, Political Thought,* p. 241.

nological civilization are far more damaging than the sins of the weak.

Pride is no harmless parlor sin for Niebuhr. In the theological meaning which he gives to it, it is the sin which corrupts the power of the strong, the wisdom of the wise, the virtue of the good, and the holiness of the saints. Pride wears many faces in man's experience, but it shows itself most characteristically in three or four forms. First, there is the pride of power. By means of acquiring more and more power, men seek to ward off their insecurity and establish their own self-sufficiency. Their will to power expresses itself in a greed which looks to wealth and physical comfort as the symbols of their mastery of the vicissitudes of nature. It seeks also "power over men" as a means of overcoming social insecurity as well as natural insecurity; and thus its by-product is always the perpetration of injustice upon others.

Secondly, there is intellectual pride. This is not just the pride of the philosopher who claims to have attained absolute truth. It is the tendency of all of us to try to obscure to ourselves and others the conditioned character of our knowledge and the degree to which our particular version of the truth is tainted by self-interest. "All human knowledge is tainted with an 'ideological' taint. It pretends to be more true than it is. It is finite knowledge, gained from a particular perspective; but it pretends to be final and ultimate knowledge." [20] The insecurity lurking under this pretension explains the fanaticism with which men are prepared to defend their systems of truth, whether in the form of a particular version of an international dispute,

[20] *The Nature and Destiny of Man,* I, 194.

the theoretical justification of racial superiority, or the cherished "denominational distinctives" of the churchman.

One of the most insidious forms of pride is moral pride, the pride of the good man who makes greater claims for his goodness than it objectively warrants. In this way it makes virtue itself the vehicle of sin. This desperate refusal to acknowledge the alloy of sin in every accomplishment of goodness is man's last-ditch attempt to justify himself. Even religion is not immune from the infection of self-righteousness. We are wrong if we assume that religion is always a good thing. On the contrary, Niebuhr insists, "it is merely a final battleground between God and man's self-esteem." [21] Thus spiritual pride is the worst kind of all, breeding the most destructive kind of intolerance, insinuating itself into our most pious practices, and tempting us to claim for our particular interests and limited viewpoints the authority of religious absolutes.

Niebuhr finds the essence of sin summarized in the biblical myth of the Fall, which he insists on taking seriously but not literally. The story of Adam in Genesis is not for him the story of a first historical man, but the story of Everyman. It is the story of each and every one of us and the way in which we inevitably succumb to the temptation to "play God" by spurning the role of freedom-in-dependence assigned to us by our Creator. In line with this interpretation, the truth of "original sin" is not to be found, as it was in traditional orthodox theology, in the notion of an inherited corruption which we all receive at birth from Adam; sin by inheritance is a contradiction in terms for Niebuhr, destroying the element of freedom and responsi-

[21] *Ibid.*, p. 200.

bility which is inherent in the very concept of sin. The idea of original sin stands rather for the inevitability and universality of sin which is occasioned by man's vain attempts to escape the anxiety of his ambiguous situation of creatureliness and self-transcendence.

A literalistic interpretation of the Genesis story of the Fall has encouraged still another theological error in Protestant thought, according to Niebuhr. In reading the story as the literal history of the first man, one finds a chronological separation between a historical period of perfection in paradise and a subsequent state of sin when man's essential nature as made in the image of God is lost. This has resulted in an exaggerated estimate of the depravity of man in his fallen state which experience clearly contradicts. A non-literal interpretation of the Adam story enables us to see the relation between man's essential nature and his sinful state as a vertical rather than a horizontal one. That is to say, the picture of original righteousness in the Genesis myth is not the description of what was true of man once upon a time before he sinned, but of what is true of him at all times in the midst of his sin. It is the symbolic representation of his essential nature from which he has fallen away, but which he has never completely lost.

In every man there is enough residual health to recognize, however dimly, the law of his life which his sin has violated. This is why "every effort to give the habits of sin the appearance of normality betrays something of the frenzy of an uneasy conscience." [22] This is the reason, also, why dishonesty and self-deception are the inevitable byproducts of sin. The self knows enough about its true

[22] *Ibid.*, p. 265.

nature to be aware that the self-deification and self-glorification involved in sin is a violation of that nature. It therefore must resort to lies and deception to hide from itself and others its own contradiction of its nature. The cloaking of egoistic behavior under frantic pretensions of virtue are thus indirect testimony to the self's awareness of the law of its essential being to which it must pay tribute, even if only in the form of desperate rationalizations of its sin. The complexity of the dynamics of sin is never fully measured, Niebuhr says, until it is realized that "evil in its most developed form is always a good which imagines itself, or pretends to be, better than it is," and that "while egoism is the driving force of sin, dishonesty is its final expression." [23] To deal realistically with the problem of sin, one must learn how to puncture these dishonest pretensions by means of which men are able skillfully to give the appearance of normality to their personal and collective sins. Few have been more adept than Niebuhr in the ability to detect these hidden hypocrisies which make it possible for individuals and groups to sustain the illusion of their own innocence.

The Social Relevance of Christian Realism: Love and Justice

"If one word had to be chosen to indicate the character of Niebuhr's work and achievement, that word would have to be 'relevance.' " [24] So writes Gordon Harland in his finely balanced interpretation of Niebuhr's thought. No

[23] *An Interpretation of Christian Ethics,* p. 97.

[24] Gordon Harland, *The Thought of Reinhold Niebuhr* (New York: Oxford University Press, 1960), p. 21.

contemporary theologian has matched Niebuhr's success in relating creatively the radical demands of the Christian gospel to the morally ambiguous situations of social and political life. This success has been achieved, in large measure, by his unusual ability to keep the realities of love and justice in continuous and fruitful tension in his thought. He has never been willing to settle for anything less than uncalculating, heedless, sacrificial *agape* as the ultimate norm and law of human existence; and yet he has been realistic enough to see that if this norm is to be made relevant to man's collective life, enslaved as it is by group egoism, it must somehow be translated into structures of justice by means of which love for neighbor is expressed, collective sin is restrained, and possibilities of community are enlarged.

The genius of Niebuhr's attempt to make the gospel relevant to the social order lies in his dual recognition of the imperative of love and the impediment of self-love at all levels of man's personal and social existence, and his insistence on taking both with equal seriousness. The following passage summarizes in an illuminating fashion the implications of this position for a Christian social ethic:

> The relevance of the law of love to the field of social institutions and collective relations is established whenever . . . religious experience bears testimony both to the law of love and to that of self-love. For to understand the law of love as a final imperative, but not to know about the persistence of the power of self-love in all of life but particularly in the collective relations of mankind, results in an idealistic ethic with no relevance to the hard realities of life. To know about the power of self-love but not to know that its power does not make it normative is to dispense with ethical standards and

fall into cynicism. But to know both the law of love as the final standard and the law of self-love as a persistent force is to enable Christians to have a foundation for a pragmatic ethic in which power and self-interest are used, beguiled, harnessed and deflected for the ultimate end of establishing the highest and most inclusive possible community of justice and order. This is the very heart of the problem of Christian politics: the readiness to use power and interest in the service of an end dictated by love and yet an absence of complacency about the evil inherent in them.[25]

Niebuhr refuses to purchase a cheap relevance to the problems of the social order by watering down the ultimate Christian norm for human life. This norm is nothing less than the *agape* of the New Testament which is utterly heedless of the claims of the self. No other norm does justice either to the constitution of human selfhood or the implications of the cross. Mutual love, which calculates the interests of the self as well as those of the other and seeks a mutually advantageous harmony, is therefore not adequate as the law of man's essential being. Only the sacrificial love which is *agape* can answer to the needs of man's essential nature, compounded as it is of both finiteness and freedom, and characterized by an indefinite capacity for self-transcendence. The self is too great to find fulfillment in itself. The law of its freedom must be a love which takes it completely out of itself. *Agape* must therefore be the final law of human existence

because every realization of the self which is motivated by concern for the self inevitably results in a narrower and more

[25] John A. Hutchison (ed.), *Christian Faith and Social Action* (New York: Charles Scribner's Sons, 1953), p. 241.

self-contained self than the freedom of the self requires. Consequently the highest forms of self-realization are those which are not intended or calculated but are the fruit of some movement of "grace" which draws the self out of itself despite itself into the love of God and the neighbor.[26]

Niebuhr's analysis of the meaning of love as the law of man's essential nature presupposes throughout the revelation of the cross, where in the crucified Christ the law of our being is embodied and clarified in a concrete historical manifestation. In Christ we are confronted with that which we essentially are and what we therefore ought to be. The norm of our life which we meet in Christ does not present us with an alien and arbitrary requirement but with the very law of our essential being. All men are to some extent aware of this law of their nature, even though they are aware of it as a lack rather than as an assured possession. They know they are created for love; but since as sinners they are corrupted by self-love, they experience the norm of their life in the form of a law whose claim and obligation places them under perpetual judgment. The uneasy conscience which results is a standing testimony to man's awareness of the law of his true self which is written in his own heart and with which he knows himself to be in conflict.

The law of love, since it is the law of man's being, is relevant to the whole of his life, including not only his more personal and intimate relationships but the social structures by means of which he establishes a wider community of justice and order. The difficulties entailed in establishing its relevance to the complexities and ambigui-

[26] *Faith and History* (New York: Charles Scribner's Sons, 1949), p. 175.

ties of the social order have tempted classical Christianity, both Protestant and Roman Catholic, to restrict its application to the realm of personal relations. This has had the disastrous consequence of removing man's social and political institutions from a relationship of tension with a transcendent norm by which the status quo is constantly brought under judgment. It has made the Christian faith virtually irrelevant to the social forces and problems which determine so pervasively man's collective existence.

If much orthodox Christianity has led to the privatization of the Christian faith and the abdication of social responsibility, it is Niebuhr's belief that modern liberal Christianity has committed the opposite error. In its commendable concern to make Christianity socially relevant, it has related the norm of love in too direct and simple fashion to the ambiguities of the social order. It has tried to use love as a strategy for social change, and in so doing it has placed undue confidence in the power of moral example and preachment to transform the structures of society. Its faith that love is a simple historical possibility is both politically unrealistic and religiously superficial. "The Christian utopians," Niebuhr writes, "think they can dispense with all structures and rules of justice simply by fulfilling the law of love. They do not realize that the law of love stands on the edge of history and not in history, that it represents an ultimate and not an immediate possibility." [27] In the cross we see that when the law of love becomes incarnate in history, it is crucified. Thus, while the love of the cross is relevant to all history, it is not *directly* relevant in the form of a strategy for historical

[27] *The Nature and Destiny of Man,* I, 298.

success. To believe that it is, is to fail to perceive the depth and persistence of sin, particularly in its collective manifestations.

One of the main reasons for modern Christianity's ineffective social witness has been its blindness to the difference between the morality of the individual and the morality of groups. The title of an epoch-making book which Niebuhr wrote in 1932 clearly dramatized this distinction: *Moral Man and Immoral Society.*[28] The thesis of the book, which has remained a central tenet of Niebuhr's social thought since that time, can be simply stated. Collective egoism is much more powerful than individual egoism and hence less susceptible to the restraints of rational and moral persuasion. This is so because groups—whether races, classes, or nations—have much less of a capacity for self-transcendence and self-criticism than do individuals. They are, moreover, much more easily tempted to idolatrous pride and the confusion of their selfish interests with absolute values than is the case with individual people. Large groups can "play God" with a much greater show of plausibility than can the lone individual.

For these reasons it is utterly fatuous to employ the same moral strategy with groups as we do with individuals. It is futile and even dangerous, for example, to exhort nations to unselfish behavior or rely on moral appeals to love in dealing with a class or race bent on exploitation. Thus, while pacifism may be a meaningful religious witness to the radical demands of the Christian norm of love, it provides no helpful guidance to the statesman seeking the adjudication of disputes between nations which cannot be

[28] (New York: Charles Scribner's Sons, 1932.)

expected to put their own interests and security in jeopardy in the face of tyranny. Likewise, labor cannot be expected to trust the benevolence of management for the securing of its rightful share of economic rewards. Nor can a racial minority be assured of freedom from discrimination by however eloquent an appeal to the conscience of the majority race.

Does this mean, then, that the law of love has no relevance for our collective existence? Not at all. It does mean, however, that if it is to become relevant, it must do so indirectly rather than directly by finding effective instruments of justice by which the neighbor in need is served; not by charming collective man by the ideal of love into an abandonment of his selfishness. This means that love is, in Niebuhr's paradoxical way of speaking, an "impossible possibility," as far as its realization in society is concerned. Given the recalcitrance of group egoism and sin, it is impossible to realize it perfectly in man's collective existence. But it *is* possible to bring social groups and institutions under the continuous judgment of the demands of *agape* and achieve a relative embodiment of it in rules and structures of justice.

It is not possible within this brief summary to expound the many ramifications of Niebuhr's extraordinarily subtle analysis of the relation between love and justice. His conception of justice is a dynamic one. Justice cannot be defined in its own terms, but only in dialectical relationship to love. Justice is love making its way in the world of complex social relationships. It is "the approximation of brotherhood under the conditions of sin." [29] It is the only

[29] *The Nature and Destiny of Man,* II, 254.

socially effective instrument for making love relevant to to the needs of man's collective life.

Neither love nor justice can maintain their integrity apart from each other. A love which tries to dispense with justice degenerates into sentimentality or contents itself with isolated deeds of philanthropy (a basket for the poor at Thanksgiving), while avoiding coming to grips with the basic structures of injustice and exploitation which subvert human welfare. A love which does not work for ever more inclusive patterns of justice in society is something less than true love.

On the other hand, any attempt to maintain justice apart from love is equally self-defeating. "Any justice which is only justice soon degenerates into something less than justice." [30] More particularly, Niebuhr says, "justice degenerates into mere order without justice if the pull of love is not upon it." [31] An essential ingredient in maintaining justice and raising it to new heights is thus the activity of love which sensitizes the conscience of individuals and groups to the needs of others. This sensitizing of the social conscience through love cannot establish and secure justice alone, without the aid of various forms of political and economic pressure wielded on behalf of disadvantaged groups; but without the leavening influence of love, whatever justice is achieved is merely a balance of power which is in constant danger of breaking down in conflict and anarchy.

The dialectical relation between love and justice implies both a positive and negative relation between the two. Thus love both fulfills and negates justice. Niebuhr shows

[30] *Moral Man and Immoral Society,* p. 258.
[31] *Faith and History,* p. 185.

the positive relation between love and justice by summarizing three ways in which systems of justice serve as instruments of brotherhood:

> Systems and principles of justice are the servants and instruments of the spirit of brotherhood in so far as they extend the sense of obligation towards the other, (a) from an immediately felt obligation, prompted by obvious need, to a continued obligation expressed in fixed principles of mutual support; (b) from a simple relation between a self and one "other" to the complex relations of the self and the "others"; and (c) finally from the obligations, discerned by the individual self, to the wider obligations which the community defines from its more impartial perspective.[32]

While every achievement of justice thus involves an approximation of brotherhood through an enhancement of responsible concern for others, it always to some extent contains contradictions of the perfect ideal of love. For one thing, no historical achievement of justice is ever completely disinterested; it always reflects the interests of particular groups or the prejudices of a particular period of history with its limitations of moral sensitivity and vision. For example, the doctrine of "separate but equal," which was long regarded in this country as a just settlement of Negro rights in education, later came to be seen by a more sensitive conscience as a rationalization of injustice. Thus justice is always capable of being redeemed and raised to new heights by love.

Justice always involves some degree of coercion which implies the loss of the spontaneity of love. "The fence and

[32] *The Nature and Destiny of Man,* II, 248.

the boundary line are the symbols of the spirit of justice." [33] As long as it is necessary to forcibly set limits upon men's interests to prevent them from taking advantage of their neighbors, only an approximation of brotherhood has been attained. But this kind of fencing in of human selfishness is essential in a sinful world if love for the neighbor is to be sincerely expressed and effectively implemented.

The Prophetic Church and Power Conflicts

Niebuhr is convinced that one of the most fundamental reasons for the church's lack of prophetic relevance is its hesitation to come to terms with the realities of power. It is an axiom of his Christian realism that justice can be established and maintained only when sufficient power is marshaled on the side of the victims of injustice to challenge the prevailing forces which would exploit their weakness. "Justice is basically dependent upon a balance of power." [34] Whenever disproportionate power falls into the hands of human beings, they wield it irresponsibly, and injustice is the inevitable result.

The church which is true to its Lord will ally itself with the weak and dispossessed, the oppressed and defenseless among men. But if it is to do this effectively, it must not abjure the responsibility of entering into the arena of social conflict in order to redress the imbalance of power which leads to unjust discrimination against the weak. It must work for the creation of instruments of political and eco-

[33] *Ibid.*, p. 252.

[34] *Christianity and Power Politics* (New York: Charles Scribner's Sons, 1952), p. 26.

nomic power capable of making the interests of the disadvantaged in society felt by the community at large.

The church has been characteristically averse to resorting to any methods of achieving justice which involve coercive pressures and political conflict. It has preferred to rely on an appeal to the goodwill of those in power establishments, hoping that moral and rational persuasion would render unnecessary what were felt to be the sub-Christian tactics of "power politics." This attempt to remain aloof from the power struggle has often been inspired by fear of the disruptive effects of controversy in the life of the church, as well as the belief that somehow power is an evil thing which Christians ought to disavow. The corollary of this belief is the conviction that politics is a "dirty business" because of its necessary dependence on the manipulation of power. "But power," Niebuhr protests, "cannot be evil of itself, unless life itself be regarded as evil. For life is power. Life is never pure form or reason. It is inherently dynamic." [35] Power as such is neither good nor evil. It depends on the use to which it is put. And a truly prophetic church will never underestimate the moral significance of power which is enlisted in the service of justice under the dictates of love. For without the bones and sinews of power, Christian love can hardly avoid becoming a harmless, flabby sentiment, lacking the effectual leverage by which it can move the principalities and powers of a sinful world.

Recently there have been hopeful indications that some sections of the church at least have laid hold upon a more vertebrate faith which does not shrink from the risks of

[35] Quoted in *The Thought of Reinhold Niebuhr*, p. 52.

controversy and conflict in order to fight for justice. This has been notably true of the church's involvement in the racial revolution, as well as its alignment with community organization programs which have been springing up in the slum areas of many of our major cities. All these forays by the church into the area of power conflicts are inspired by a Niebuhrian style of Christian realism.

Community organization movements, such as Saul Alinsky's Industrial Areas Foundation, have come under considerable criticism by churchmen who object to methods of bringing submerged resentments into the open and fostering open conflict with the economic and political power structures of the city. In a recent article John C. Bennett has observed that "most of the criticism of community development movements is what might be called pre-Niebuhrian." While not condoning all the methods employed by such movements, he goes on to express a characteristically Niebuhrian judgment of their significance for the church: "One cannot escape from sin by refusing to relate oneself to movements that seek to develop the power of self-defense among the powerless. One becomes involved in some evil by-products, but one should also count up the evil by-products of refusing to do this: hypocrisy on one side, apathy on the other, and the injustice that pervades it all." [36]

Long before the days of freedom marches, sit-ins, bus boycotts and rent strikes, Niebuhr saw the theological and political wisdom in such methods of nonviolent resistance. In 1932 he wrote: "Nonviolent coercion and resistance . . . is a type of coercion which offers the largest

[36] "The Church and Power Conflicts" in *Christianity and Crisis,* March 22, 1965, p. 50.

opportunities for a harmonious relationship with the moral and rational factors in social life." [37] It combines appeals to conscience and to self-interest, to love and to self-love, which hold out the greatest possibilities for Negro emancipation. Such emancipation would never come, however, "merely by trusting in the moral sense of the white race." [38] "However large the number of individual white men who will identify themselves completely with the Negro cause," Niebuhr prophesied, "the white race in America will not admit the Negro to equal rights if it is not forced to do so." [39]

The uncanny accuracy of Niebuhr's predictions is the product of his theological realism which finds the roots of race prejudice not so much in man's ignorance as in his idolatry, that is, in "his partly conscious and partly unconscious effort to make himself, his race, and his culture God." [40] It is one manifestation of man's abortive attempt to escape from the anxiety and insecurity of his human existence. "Race bigotry is, in short, one form of original sin." As such, it "must be broken by repentance, and not merely by enlightenment." [41]

If racial pride and prejudice is of the very essence of original sin, then the church has in its armory the weapon to attack it at its roots—the contrition-producing preaching of the gospel. It is a tragic irony of the history of the American church, particularly in its southern revivalistic branches, that its legalistic preoccupation with the often

[37] *Moral Man and Immoral Society*, pp. 250-51.
[38] *Ibid.*, p. 252.
[39] *Ibid.*, p. 253.
[40] D. B. Robertson (ed.), *Love and Justice* (Philadelphia: Westminster Press, 1957), p. 129.
[41] *Ibid.*, p. 128.

picayune sins of the individual has resulted in an almost total failure to stimulate repentance for collective sins such as racial prejudice and discrimination. The preaching of a prophetic church will make concrete and inescapable to its members the true nature of race prejudice as one of the most venial forms of man's basic sin of pride. To the degree to which it is successful, it will be making what Niebuhr feels is its most important contribution, namely, "to present the national community with a greater number of truly contrite souls, truly 'emancipated' of race prejudice, who express their emancipation partly in the contrite recognition of the remnant of pride that remains in the souls of even the emancipated." [42]

The church, however, cannot be content simply to try to eradicate prejudice by inducing repentance. If the Negro neighbor is truly to be loved, he must be protected from the ravages of those who would discriminate against him and rob him of his rightful heritage of equal justice. The churchman who counsels the Negro to wait for the guaranteeing of that heritage until more hearts are changed by the preaching of the gospel betrays an appalling insensitivity and lovelessness. The church which would serve its Lord by meeting the needs of "the least of these," his brethren, must enter the lists of social and political conflicts and pressures in a relentless quest for instruments of power and legality by means of which "man's inhumanity to man" is restrained. This will mean, among other things, lobbying for legislation to establish and fortify justice and equal opportunity in voting, employment, housing, and education. In answer to a favorite pious

[42] *Ibid.*, p. 129.

dodge by those who would criticize the church's involvement in such activities, Kyle Haselden has written some devastating sentences which have a strong Niebuhrian ring:

> It will still be said, "You cannot legislate morals"; to this saying the state should answer, "We are not trying to legislate your morals; but we can restrain your immoralities." Laws are passed not to make bad people good, but to make innocent people safe. . . . No law, not even the law of God, will compel us to love the Negro; but the proper law, properly enforced, will reduce the effects of hatred, contempt, and greed upon the life of the Negro. . . . Enforced justice puts the visible sin of man under judgment and restraint; it is the compromise which love makes with a sinful world.[43]

The necessity of compromise in making love relevant to a sinful world has been a perennial stumbling block in the way of a meaningful and effective Christian social witness. Christians have been too frequently prone to run from the rough-and-tumble of political conflict in an effort to protect their own personal sanctification and build an island of personal purity uncontaminated by moral compromise of any kind. This perfectionist tendency is not only productive of social irresponsibility but is, Niebuhr believes, a denial of a basic tenet of Reformation Christianity, the doctrine of justification by faith. His description of the meaning of that doctrine for Christian social involvement is a remarkable example of his ability to make abstract theological truth relevant to the concrete issues of life:

[43] Kyle Haselden, *The Racial Problem in Christian Perspective* (New York: Harper & Row, 1959), pp. 111-12.

Justification by faith in the realm of justice means that we will not regard the pressures and counter pressures, the tensions, the overt and the covert conflicts by which justice is achieved and maintained, as normative in the absolute sense; but neither will we ease our conscience by seeking to escape from involvement in them. We will know that we cannot purge ourselves of the sin and guilt in which we are involved by the moral ambiguities of politics without also disavowing responsibility for the creative possibilities of justice.[44]

The Christian who is sustained by the biblical truth implicit in the doctrine of justification by faith knows that in the final analysis nothing that he can do by securing for himself a ledge of purity above the rushing, muddy waters of life can earn his standing in the sight of God. He knows that he is justified by grace alone. In this conviction he is freed for responsible involvement in the morally ambiguous situations and conflicts of the social order. Trusting in the forgiveness of God, where love must run the risk of compromise to be relevant to human need, he is delivered alike from illusions about his own righteousness and despair of the creative possibilities of God's continuing work of love in the world. His is the "spiritual relaxation without which all moral striving generates a stinking sweat of self-righteousness and an alternation of fanatic illusions and fretful disillusionments." [45] The "nonchalance of faith"—this is the ultimate source and secret of the morale of the Christian realist in his tireless search for more adequate ways of making the love of the cross relevant to the needs of a sinful world.

[44] *The Nature and Destiny of Man,* II, 284.

[45] *Reflections on the End of an Era* (New York: Charles Scribner's Sons, 1934), p. 296.

VI

DIETRICH BONHOEFFER
WORLDLINESS AS A CHRISTIAN STANCE

Perhaps no name appears more frequently in the rapidly escalating discussions concerning the renewal of the church than the name of Dietrich Bonhoeffer. In a recent book Bishop John A. T. Robinson has gone so far as to call him "the John the Baptist of the New Reformation." [1] Twenty years after his martyrdom at the hands of a Nazi hanging squad, the prophetic import of his revolutionary ideas are for the first time being widely recognized and assimilated in the life of the church.

During the postwar years the dramatic story of Bonhoeffer's career as a courageous resistance fighter and Christian martyr kindled the imagination of considerable numbers of college and seminary students who found in him the exemplar of a robust and earthy brand of "worldly Christianity." They found in him one whose story, as Reinhold Niebuhr once said, "belongs to the modern Acts of the Apostles." [2] The earliest of his books to be translated

[1] *The New Reformation?* (Philadelphia: Westminster Press, 1965), p. 23.

[2] Quoted in John D. Godsey, *The Theology of Dietrich Bonhoeffer* (Philadelphia: Westminster Press, 1960), p. 203.

into English, *The Cost of Discipleship,* for which he later provided the postscript of a supreme sacrifice, challenged them with the model of a more strenuous and demanding form of Christian life and witness than the church had customarily provided.

More recently, Bonhoeffer's stature as a highly sophisticated theologian of major significance has been increasingly recognized. Theologians and church leaders have turned particularly to the enigmatic fragments of his later work for clues as to how to rethink the church's mission to the radically secularized world of the twentieth century. His program for a "religionless Christianity" to match the needs of a secular age has given aid and comfort to some who would prematurely write off the institutional church as a viable expression of the Christian faith in the modern world. It is highly doubtful that Bonhoeffer himself would have approved of such a use of his ideas. It is true that in his prison letters he predicted that within a generation "the form of the Church will have changed beyond recognition." [3] But there is no evidence that he ever abandoned a lifelong passionate commitment to the church, a commitment which remained unbroken even throughout the years of agonizing and often fruitless struggle to preserve her from apostasy under the Nazi regime.

It is a mistake, therefore, to think of Bonhoeffer as a secular theologian in contrast to a church theologian. His theologizing was from beginning to end a sustained effort to elucidate the way in which Christ takes form in his body the church as an anticipation of the formation of all men into their true humanity. John D. Godsey, the

[3] *Prisoner for God* (New York: The Macmillan Company, 1953), p. 140.

author of the first full-scale treatment of Bonhoeffer's thought in English, finds his concentration on the concrete life of the church and its mission in the world to be his distinctive contribution among contemporary theologians. In a glowing appraisal, he writes:

> In Bonhoeffer we have a theologian whose thought is as Christocentric as that of Barth, who raised the question of the communication of the gospel as sharply as Rudolf Bultmann, who was led to take the problems of our pragmatic, problem-solving, technological world as seriously as Reinhold Niebuhr, but who, more than any of these men, thought from the perspective of the concrete church. Not that these men are not church theologians, but Bonhoeffer somehow more consistently made the body of Christ the center of his concern and the *terminus a quo* of his thinking. He challenged the church to be the church by bringing into line its word and its act, its faith and order and its life and work.[4]

A loyal son of the church, Bonhoeffer bequeathed to it not only the radiant witness of a martyr's death but the theological deposits of a disciplined and creative mind, reflection upon which is opening up new possibilities for Christian renewal in our time.

From Classroom to Concentration Camp

Of Bonhoeffer it is perhaps more true than is the case with most theologians that the development of his theological ideas paralleled his own personal involvement in the ideological struggles of his time and his successive roles in the life and ministry of the church. That this should be so is

[4] *Theology of Dietrich Bonhoeffer*, p. 17.

consistent with his understanding of the nature of the theological enterprise. Toward the end of his life Bonhoeffer was to elaborate a contextualist understanding of ethics. Actually, as he conceived of its function and practiced it, the discipline of theology as a whole was inescapably contextual. Theology does not consist of the delineation of abstract propositions of truth unrelated to life, but of a continuing attempt to disclose the implications of the revelation in Christ for life in concrete terms.

Bonhoeffer's close friend and official biographer, Eberhard Bethge, has observed that Bonhoeffer saw concreteness as an attribute of revelation itself, since God has, as it were, concretized himself in Jesus Christ. It is not, therefore, something that needs to be artificially added by the homiletical expertise of the preacher or the religious magic of the apologist. As far as the Christian message is concerned, "there is no treasure at all except the one which, on being discovered, at the same moment bursts with application by itself." [5] The task of theology, then, is simply to expose the concrete content of revelation to view, so that its application to life becomes self-evident.

Godsey has remarked that "the most impressive thing about Dietrich Bonhoeffer is the way in which his own life provides the commentary on his theology." [6] This is so because his theology, much as was the case with Niebuhr, was forged out of the various experiential involvements of his own life. His theological pilgrimage reflects very clearly his successive callings as teacher, pastor, ecumenical churchman, and political activist. From classroom to con-

[5] "The Challenge of Dietrich Bonhoeffer's Life and Theology" in *The Chicago Theological Seminary Register,* February, 1961, p. 7.

[6] *Theology of Dietrich Bonhoeffer,* p. 281.

centration camp, Bonhoeffer's theological activity took the form of a relentless quest for the concrete nature of the Christian message.

The exigencies of Bonhoeffer's own personal history, as he responded with great sensitivity to the crises engulfing his church and his nation, produced three clearly discernible phases in his theological development. In his 1961 lectures at Chicago Theological Seminary, Bethge identified these three periods and their dates as follows: (1) foundation: the quest for the concrete nature of the message (1927-33); (2) concentration: the narrow pass for Christianity (1933-40); and (3) liberation: Christianity without religion (1940-45).[7]

The first period was a predominantly theoretical period in which he studied and taught at the University of Berlin and in which he hammered out the dogmatic foundations on the basis of which his later theological explorations were launched. The second period was more of a pastoral one in which he entered actively into the German church struggle, served German-speaking churches in London, gave himself increasingly to the leadership of the ecumenical movement, and finally led a small underground seminary for preachers of the Confessing Church. The final period was a political one in which he assumed the ambiguous role of a member of the resistance movement, participating in a plot against the life of Hitler for which he was imprisoned and eventually executed.

The first period produced two of his most sophisticated works of theological scholarship—a doctoral dissertation written at the age of twenty-one entitled *Sanctorum Com-*

[7] "Challenge of Dietrich Bonhoeffer's Life and Theology," p. 3.

munio (The Communion of Saints),[8] which Karl Barth once called "a theological miracle," and *Act and Being,*[9] a book written to qualify for a teaching post at the University of Berlin. These works bore the stamp of Barth's influence, even though they took vigorous issue with certain conclusions of his dialectical theology. Bonhoeffer was especially critical of Barth's view of God as "Wholly Other" and his atomizing of revelation into contingent acts which, while removing it from the possibility of human control, at the same time destroyed its continuity in human history and its genuine entry into human existence. In a statement in which Bonhoeffer anticipates in a remarkable way Barth's own modification of his earlier views in *The Humanity of God,* he says: "God is not free *of* man but *for* man. Christ is the Word of his freedom. God is *there,* which is to say: not in eternal non-objectivity but . . . 'haveable,' graspable in His Word within the Church." [10]

His earlier book, *Sanctorum Communio,* had shown how God's revelation becomes concrete and graspable in the church defined as "Christ existing as community." Bonhoeffer wrote in a quite realistic sense of "Christ existing as the church." [11] As the body of Christ, the church exists as a community of love which God has created to incarnate the principle of vicarious action. Christ's "real presence" in the church is seen in the way in which this principle becomes operative in its members' relationships with one another, in their "being for one another" as well

[8] (New York: Harper & Row, 1963.)
[9] (London: Collins, 1962.)
[10] *Act and Being,* pp. 90-91.
[11] *The Communion of Saints,* p. 146.

as their "being with one another." [12] Thus the church is the concrete sociological community, the "collective person," in which the revelation of God takes form as a reconciled and reconciling fellowship of persons, and man's separation from God and his fellows is overcome in Christ.

This identification of the church with the continuing presence of Christ as community had its obvious dangers of which Bonhoeffer was very much aware. To make the identification of Christ and his church absolute was, of course, to commit idolatry. This danger became a very real one during the German church struggle of the 1930's. To combat it, Bonhoeffer devoted himself during the second phase of his theological development to an increasing emphasis on the lordship of Christ over his body the church. The two most important writings of this period, *The Cost of Discipleship* and *Life Together,* represent a call to costly obedience and instruction in Christian discipline as the only protection against the imminent threat of the church of Christ becoming the church of Antichrist.

The challenge to the integrity of the church under Nazi pressure came to a head in a series of ominous events in 1933 following Hitler's accession to power. Bonhoeffer almost immediately made his protest, attacking the idolatry implicit in the Nazi "leadership principle" in a radio broadcast which was cut off before its completion by government monitors. When legislation was passed disqualifying anyone of Jewish ancestry from holding office in the state, and when the German church applied these Aryan laws to ecclesiastical appointments, Bonhoeffer resigned his teaching post and went to London, where he served as

[12] *Ibid.,* p. 126.

a pastor for the next two years. In 1935, on the urgent call of the Confessing Church (the group of Christians who held out against the Nazi-dominated Reich Church), Bonhoeffer returned to organize and lead a small seminary at Finkenwalde. An incident which occurred there typifies the Bonhoeffer of this period. Some of his students came to him with the suggestion that it was poor strategy for them to continue to remain outside the Reich Church, thereby losing the chance to occupy the best pulpits and extend their influence more widely. They reminded Bonhoeffer of all the true sermons they could preach if only they had the proper state credentials. The directness of his reply left little room for argument then or now: "One act of obedience is better than a hundred sermons." [13]

The second period of Bonhoeffer's life and theology came to an end on the eve of World War II with his abortive trip to the United States for a lecture tour on the invitation of Reinhold Niebuhr and other American friends. In 1930-31 he had spent a year there studying at Union Theological Seminary. This time he had barely set foot on American soil when his conscience began to chide him. A letter written to Reinhold Niebuhr conveying his decision to return immediately to Germany reveals the true mettle of the man:

I have come to the conclusion that I have made a mistake in coming to America. I must live through this difficult period of our national history with the Christian people of Germany. I shall have no right to participate in the reconstruction of Christian life in Germany after the war if I do not share the

[13] Edwin H. Robertson (ed.), *No Rusty Swords* (New York: Harper & Row, 1965), p. 18.

trials of this time with my people. . . . Christians in Germany will face the terrible alternative of either willing the defeat of their nation in order that Christian civilisation may survive, or willing the victory of their nation and thereby destroying our civilisation. I know which of these alternatives I must choose; *but I cannot make that choice in security.*[14]

With that decision, Bonhoeffer set his feet on the road which in the five brief years remaining to him made his biography a glowing commentary on *The Cost of Discipleship*. During his middle period, he had been concerned about the faithfulness and integrity of the church in its form as a gathered community. Now he was to think through the implications of its mission as a people of God scattered in the world. It was during this final period that he developed his concept of "worldliness" as the only stance appropriate for the Christian who would be faithful to his Lord.

While some of the rather startling innovations in his thought in this final phase could not have been anticipated on the basis of his earlier work, it is probably a mistake to assume that they represent a radical break from his previous theological position. Martin Marty raises the question as to whether such an assumption is, among other things, psychologically tenable: "Does 'a very sophisticated theologian' suddenly move out of his mentally furnished apartment; can he, as it were, 'jump out of his skin'?" [15] Whether one sees the continuity between the late and early Bonhoeffer in terms of a quest for new forms of concrete-

[14] *Ibid.*, p. 22.

[15] Martin E. Marty (ed.), *The Place of Bonhoeffer* (New York: Association Press, 1962), p. 16.

ness of the Word of God, as Bethge has done, or in terms of the expansion of his understanding of the implications of Christology, as Godsey has suggested, the continuity is undoubtedly there.

Bonhoeffer himself was never prepared to repudiate the validity of his earlier work, though he was quite conscious of the radical newness of some of his later proposals. Writing in one of his prison letters about *The Cost of Discipleship,* he expressed misgivings about his tendency at that time toward a religiously introverted form of Christian piety. "Today I can see the dangers of this book, though I am prepared to stand by what I wrote." [16]

There is a good deal to be said for Godsey's schema, according to which Bonhoeffer's thought developed under the impact of a progressively deepening awareness of the total meaning of Jesus Christ and the scope of his dominion and claim. Thus the three periods of his theological pilgrimage may be characterized in terms of their main emphases as follows: "During the first period his thought centered on *Jesus Christ as the revelational reality of the church.* During the second period his emphasis was upon *Jesus Christ as Lord over the church.* In the third period Bonhoeffer concentrated his attention upon *Jesus Christ as the Lord over the world."* [17]

In one of his last letters from prison Bonhoeffer wrote to his friend that "I discovered and am still discovering up to this very moment that it is only by living completely in this world that one learns to believe." [18] His own experience of total immersion in the risks and ambiguities

[16] *Prisoner for God,* p. 168.
[17] *Theology of Dietrich Bonhoeffer,* p. 266.
[18] *Prisoner for God,* p. 169.

of life in the world went hand in hand with the formulation of a radically christological view of Christian ethics and some daring, though fragmentary, suggestions for a theology of the secular. His *Ethics* is a compilation of scattered writings produced during the period from 1940 to 1943 when he was working for the underground resistance movement under the guise of a civilian employee of the German Military Intelligence Service, and which were recovered after his death from a variety of hiding places and published in 1949. Arrested on April 5, 1943, Bonhoeffer spent the last two years of his life in two Berlin prisons and the concentration camp at Buchenwald. His legacy to the Christian world during this period consists of letters and papers smuggled out of the prison by friendly guards and published eventually in the United States under the title *Prisoner for God.* These documents reveal not only a remarkable portrait of Christian faith and fortitude under trial but a series of sometimes puzzling, but always provocative, fragments of theological reflection with which theologians are still trying to come to terms.

Christ and the Mandate for Christian Worldliness

It is because Bonhoeffer's theology is radically incarnational that it drives inexorably toward worldliness. While it took the catalyst of a costly personal exposure to the harsh realities of the secular world to make it explicit, this mandate for a "worldly Christianity" was implicit in his christocentric approach from the beginning. Bonhoeffer's theology makes it unmistakably clear to the church of the twentieth-century that "worldliness as a Christian stance" is an imperative rooted in the gospel of the incarnation.

The Christian worldliness of which Bonhoeffer speaks, it goes without saying, has nothing to do with "the shallow this-worldliness of the enlightened, of the busy, the comfortable or the lascivious." [19] The worldliness which he recommends for the Christian is a holy worldliness—a worldliness compatible only with a costly discipleship, a worldliness which is always suffused with the knowledge of death and resurrection. "When Christ calls a man, He bids him come and die." [20] So wrote Bonhoeffer in 1937, little realizing how prophetic he was concerning his own personal future. In 1944, a few months before his martyrdom, he was defining worldliness as the kind of life in which we take everything in our stride "with all its duties and problems, its successes and failures, its experiences and helplessness" and in which "we throw ourselves utterly in the arms of God and participate in his sufferings in the world and watch with Christ in Gethsemane." [21]

One is bound to misunderstand Bonhoeffer's discussions of Christian worldliness in the prison letters unless one sees them against the background of his impassioned polemic against "cheap grace" in *The Cost of Discipleship*. There he provided a withering criticism of modern evangelical churches who dispense grace on such cheap and easy terms that it amounts to "the justification of sin without the justification of the sinner." [22] Such churches pride themselves on holding a correct doctrine of grace and justification, intellectual assent to which is accepted as an ade-

[19] *Ibid.*, p. 168.

[20] *The Cost of Discipleship* (New York: The Macmillan Company, 1958), p. 73.

[21] *Prisoner for God*, p. 169.

[22] *The Cost of Discipleship*, p. 37.

quate substitute for the true life of discipleship. And so a man can reason:

> I can go and sin as much as I like, and rely on this grace to forgive me, for after all the world is justified in principle by grace. I can therefore cling to my bourgeois secular existence, and remain as I was before, but with the added assurance that the grace of God will cover me. . . . The upshot of it all is that my only duty as a Christian is to escape from the world for an hour or so on a Sunday morning and go to Church to be assured that my sins are all forgiven. I need no longer try to follow Christ, for cheap grace, the bitterest foe of all true discipleship, has freed me from that.[23]

Bonhoeffer is alarmed by this reduction of the gospel to a proclamation of and assent to a general truth about justification and forgiveness of sins, mainly because it adds up to a denial of the incarnation. The gospel is not the declaration of a general religious truth, but God's costly identification with us in the concrete realities of our mundane existence. And we cannot really appropriate the benefits of the incarnation without entering into it existentially and sharing in the sufferings of God which it entails. That is why Bonhoeffer is constrained to say: "The only man who has the right to say that he is justified by grace alone is the man who has left all to follow Christ."[24]

Otherworldliness is a perennial temptation for weak Christians who cannot stand the rigors of a costly discipleship in the world. "We are otherworldly," Bonhoeffer wrote as far back as 1923, "ever since we hit upon the devious trick of being religious, yes even 'Christian,' at

[23] *Ibid.*, pp. 44-45.
[24] *Ibid.*, p. 45.

the expense of the earth. . . . Whenever life begins to become oppressive and troublesome a person just leaps into the air with a bold kick and soars relieved and unencumbered into so-called eternal fields." [25] But such religious escapism has no mandate from Christ. "He does not lead man in a religious flight from this world to other worlds beyond; rather, he gives him back to the earth as its loyal son." [26]

The christological justification of worldliness as a Christian stance was developed more fully by Bonhoeffer in his *Ethics.* Here he sees Christ as the revelation of ultimate reality, the origin and goal of all existence, apart from which we cannot really understand either God or the world. When we take Christ as our point of departure, we are driven to the conclusion that in him God and the world are inseparably joined together.

> In Christ we are offered the possibility of partaking in the reality of God and in the reality of the world, but not in the one without the other. The reality of God discloses itself only by setting me entirely in the reality of the world, and when I encounter the reality of the world it is already sustained, accepted and reconciled in the reality of God.[27]

Since in Christ the unity of God and the world is established, the church is in error whenever it thinks in terms of two static spheres, the secular and the Christian, as conflicting and irreconcilable antitheses. "What God has joined together, let no man put asunder." Bonhoeffer

[25] "Thy Kingdom Come" in John D. Godsey's *Preface to Bonhoeffer* (Philadelphia: Fortress Press, 1965), p. 28.

[26] *Ibid.,* p. 29.

[27] *Ethics* (New York: The Macmillan Company, 1962), p. 61.

would pronounce these words of consummation over the marriage bond which has been forged between God and the world as a consequence of Christ's reconciling work. "Just as in Christ the reality of God entered into the reality of the world, so, too, is that which is Christian to be found only in that which is of the world, the 'supernatural' only in the natural, the holy only in the profane, and the revelational only in the rational." [28]

This is not to say that these opposites are made identical. Bonhoeffer is not dissolving the Christian into the secular in the manner of modern secularism. He is trying to preserve a "polemical unity" between the two which denies their independence from one another, while recognizing the relative autonomy of each. Just as Luther appealed in the name and with the help of the secular for a better Christianity, "so, too, today, when Christianity is employed as a polemical weapon against the secular, this must be done in the name of a better secularity and above all it must not lead back to a static predominance of the spiritual sphere as an end in itself." [29]

To see God and the world united in Christ is to recognize the lordship of Christ over all creation. Because everything in creation owes its existence and meaning to Jesus Christ, his lordship over it does not represent the imposition of an arbitrary and alien law. "The commandment of Jesus Christ, the living Lord, sets creation free for the fulfillment of the law which is its own, that is to say, the law which is inherent in it by virtue of its having its origin, its goal and its essence in Jesus Christ." [30]

[28] *Ibid.*, p. 65.
[29] *Ibid.*
[30] *Ibid.*, p. 264.

The lordship of Christ over the world assumes concrete form in four mandates: labor, marriage, government, and the church. God wills that these various realms of human existence be directed, each in its own way, toward Christ as their divinely appointed end. All four mandates have been imposed on all men so that "there can be no retreating from a 'secular' into a 'spiritual' sphere." [31] The Christian life is expressed as much under the mandates of labor, marriage, and government as under the mandate of the church. Nor do any of these mandates have any intrinsic superiority over the others, justifying, for example, the domination of government by the church, or the family by government.

> The commandment of Jesus Christ does indeed rule over Church, family, culture and government; but it does so while at the same time setting each of these mandates free for the fulfillment of its own allotted functions. Jesus Christ's claim to lordship, which is proclaimed by the Church, means at the same time the emancipation of family, culture and government for the realization of their own essential character which has its foundation in Christ.[32]

This freedom of secular institutions from interference with their God-given functions, Bonhoeffer warns, should discourage all attempts to christianize them by subordinating them to the church. God's will for the state is not that it be made over in the image of the church, but that it *be* a state, discharging the functions of administration of justice and preservation of order assigned to it by the Creator. Similarly, God's will for the university is not that

[31] *Ibid.*, p. 73.
[32] *Ibid.*, p. 264.

it be an "arm of the church," providing the latter with opportunities for indoctrination and evangelism, but that it *be* a university, pursuing faithfully its essentially "worldly" task of honest and untrammeled inquiry after truth. "The purpose and aim of the dominion of Christ is not to make the worldly order godly or to subordinate it to the Church but to set it free for true worldliness." [33]

It is only on the basis of a proper christological understanding, Bonhoeffer insists, that the Christian is able to take seriously the structures and responsibilities of the secular order, respecting their integrity and necessity as an expression of the universal lordship of Christ, while avoiding the temptation to deify them. He can respect the relative autonomy of the secular, not because the secular is important in itself but because it is important in relation to Christ as the sphere of his lordship. In the cross God speaks both his No and his Yes to the world, both his word of judgment and his word of grace. In the light of this ultimate word of God to man, the Christian must take the world seriously but not uncritically. He must give the secular its due, not for its own sake but for the sake of Christ.

The Ultimate and the Penultimate

This paradoxical nature of true Christian worldliness receives one of its most fruitful expositions in Bonhoeffer's description of the relation between the ultimate and the penultimate, "the last things and the things before the last." For Bonhoeffer, the ultimate is God's justification of the sinner, the breaking into man's history of his act

[33] *Ibid.*, p. 294.

and word of grace in Jesus Christ. This justifying word of God is final and ultimate in two senses: first, in the qualitative sense, that it is God's own free word which pronounces judgment on everything penultimate which precedes it, and is not therefore guaranteed or necessitated by any human methods which we may devise to bring about its utterance; second, in the quantitative sense, that it is "always preceded by something penultimate, some action, suffering, movement, volition, defeat, uprising, entreaty or hope, that is to say, in a quite genuine sense by a span of time, at the end of which it stands." [34]

Two extreme solutions to the problem of relating the ultimate to the penultimate are rejected by Bonhoeffer as leading to the destruction of genuine Christian worldliness. There is a radical solution which sees only the ultimate as important and writes off everything penultimate as an enemy of Christ. It is concerned only with preaching the gospel of grace and drawing men directly into the ultimate, while abdicating all penultimate responsibilities in the world. This kind of solution is epitomized by those who exhort the church and its ministry to "stick to preaching the gospel, and stop meddling in politics." The other solution is the way of compromise which sets the ultimate on one side and deals with the penultimate on its own terms, thus removing it from the possibility of any transcendent criticism or judgment. This way of relating the ultimate to the penultimate, then, becomes a means of sanctioning the status quo, "an eternal justification for things as they are." [35]

The stance of Christian worldliness, which draws its in-

[34] *Ibid.*, p. 83.
[35] *Ibid.*, p. 86.

spiration not only from the incarnation but the cross and resurrection as well, will recognize the limited insight into truth represented by both these extremes, while avoiding the divorce of the ultimate from the penultimate which they arrive at from their completely different starting points. It will give the penultimate its due, but only for the sake of the ultimate. It will take the penultimate seriously because only in this context does it look for the revelation of the ultimate. At the same time, it will never regard the penultimate as the "last word," but only "the word before the last," which receives both its legitimation and the definition of its limits from the last word which God pronounces in Jesus Christ.

If this last word is to be heard by men, proper care must be taken for the penultimate words and acts which lead up to it and prepare the way for it. "You cannot and must not speak the last word before you have spoken the next to last." [36] "For the sake of the ultimate the penultimate must be preserved. Any arbitrary destruction of the penultimate will do serious injury to the ultimate." [37]

While Christ will come to men in his own time and in his own way, there are conditions of the heart and of the world which impede the reception of his grace and render faith difficult. This means that for the Christian there is the task of preparing the way for Christ. Concretely, this is done by helping men to be truly men and truly good. Everything which frustrates the fulfillment of the penultimate realities of manhood and goodness is a barrier to the breaking in of the ultimate reality which is God's word of reconciliation in Christ. This is why feeding

[36] *Prisoner for God,* p. 79.
[37] *Ethics,* p. 92.

the hungry, sheltering the homeless, bringing justice to the dispossessed and freedom to the enslaved are not extracurricular activities for Christians; they are essential expressions of an evangelical mandate. To labor for civil rights, to engage in political struggle in behalf of the disadvantaged and voiceless members of society, to do battle with ignorance, poverty, and disease—these penultimate involvements cannot be dismissed as secular and hence "unspiritual." They are essential "spiritual" activities insofar as they clear the way for faith and make it easier to accept the grace of Christ and acknowledge his lordship.

Every attempt to make men more truly human is a Christian act, even though the name of Christ is not explicitly invoked.[38] In fact, Bonhoeffer was characteristically suspicious of any tendency to invoke the Christian label too glibly and offer Christian solutions too facilely. In a revealing passage he writes:

So that this may become quite clear, let us ask why it is that precisely in thoroughly grave situations, for instance when I am with someone who has suffered a bereavement, I often decide to adopt a "penultimate" attitude, particularly when I am dealing with Christians, remaining silent as a sign that I share in the bereaved man's helplessness in the face of such a grievous event, and not speaking the biblical words of comfort which are, in fact, known to me and available to me. Why am I often unable to open my mouth, when I ought to give expression to the ultimate? And why, instead, do I decide on an expression of thoroughly penultimate human solidarity?

[38] A recent major contribution to Christian ethics by Paul Lehmann bears the unmistakable stamp of Bonhoeffer's influence in its emphasis on "What God is doing to make and to keep human life *human* in the world." *Ethics in a Christian Context* (New York: Harper & Row, 1963), p. 99.

Is it from mistrust of the power of the ultimate word? Is it from fear of men? Or is there some good positive reason for such an attitude, namely, that my knowledge of the word, my having it at my finger-tips, in other words my being, so to speak, spiritually master of the situation, bears only the appearance of the ultimate, but is in reality itself something entirely penultimate? Does one not in some cases, by remaining deliberately in the penultimate, perhaps point all the more genuinely to the ultimate, which God will speak in His own time (though indeed even then through a human mouth)? [39]

Bonhoeffer's concern to give the penultimate its due in the Christian life is even more pronounced in his letters from prison. Here he warns against a false piety which is always trying to live at the level of the ultimate and is restrained by a pseudoreligiousness from enjoying God's gifts in the penultimate. "I am sure," he writes, "we ought to love God in our *lives* and in all the blessings he sends us. . . . Speaking frankly, to long for the transcendent when you are in your wife's arms is, to put it mildly, a lack of taste, and it is certainly not what God expects of us. We ought to find God and love him in the blessings he sends us. If he pleases to grant us some overwhelming earthly bliss, we ought not to try and be more religious than God himself." [40] This last reference suggests the way in which the ultimate-penultimate distinction provided for Bonhoeffer the basis for his polemic against religiosity as a false perversion of the relationship between God and man, and God and the world, established in Jesus Christ. God's way with men is not to lift them out of the penultimate

[39] *Ethics,* pp. 84-85.
[40] *Prisoner for God,* p. 86.

into the ultimate, not to provide an escape from the secular into the religious, but to redeem both the penultimate and the secular.

Responsible Christian Decision and the Form of Christ

Much of our discussion of Bonhoeffer's conception of the ultimate and the penultimate has been on a rather abstract level. We must now ask how the ultimate is related to the penultimate in terms of the concrete decisions of the Christian in his attempt to discern the will of God and translate it into worldly terms. This brings us to the very heart of the problem of ethics.

The problem and its solution are seen by Bonhoeffer, as we might expect, in christological terms. A question which kept coming back to him as he meditated in his prison cell may be allowed to stand as a statement of the problem: "What *is* Christianity, and indeed what *is* Christ, for us today?" [41] The solution to the ethical problem may be summarily indicated by the phrase "conformation with Christ." Christian ethics is concerned not with "what is good once and for all, but the way in which Christ takes form among us here and now." [42]

This basic motif of Bonhoeffer's ethics is not a summons to "be like Jesus" in the sense that we start with a set of notions as to what Jesus was like and then try to emulate them in our own lives. It is a call, rather, to a kind of conformation with the incarnate, crucified, and risen Christ which may assume quite different manifestations and take

[41] *Ibid.*, p. 122.
[42] *Ethics*, p. 23.

on quite different guises than were apparent in the Jesus of history. Conformation with Christ means the undergoing of "a 'metamorphosis,' a complete inward transmutation of one's previous form, a 'renewing of the mind' (Rom. 12:2), a 'walking as children of light' (Eph. 5:8)."[43] It is the process of being formed into a new mode of existence in which one becomes "a real man" even as God took the form of a real man in Christ; in which one stands humbly and penitently under the sentence and judgment of God "in the likeness of the Crucified"; and in which one stands as "a new man before God" in conformation with the Risen One.

The church is the locus in history in which this transformation takes place. "The Church is nothing but a section of humanity in which Christ has really taken form." As Bonhoeffer sees it, the church "has essentially nothing whatever to do with the so-called religious functions of man, but with the whole man in his existence in the world with all its implications. What matters in the Church is not religion but the form of Christ, and its taking form amidst a band of men."[44] This form is the proper form of all humanity. Therefore the formation into the image of Christ which takes place in the church takes place as an example and substitute for all men. Thus the church is the vanguard of God's renewing activity in the world by which he is bringing men into "the measure of the stature of the fulness of Christ" (Eph. 4:13).

This accent on the concrete formation of life after the pattern of Christ leads to a view of Christian ethics in

[43] *Ibid.,* p. 162.
[44] *Ibid.,* p. 21.

which abstract principles and legalistic definitions of good have no place. Largely under the inspiration of Bonhoeffer's germinal insights, a position known as "contextualism" has become widely influential in the field of Christian ethics in recent years. This position rejects the use of laws and principles as the final arbiters of Christian decision and action. It places the onus of Christian decision on the individual believer who must discern the will of God afresh in each new situation in the light of the unique complex of factors which define the context of his decision.

Bonhoeffer's contextualism is a position which takes with equal seriousness the implications of faith and the givenness of facts. It grounds responsible Christian decision not in a set of preestablished rules and principles, but in the situation of dynamic encounter and tension which is created when a man surrenders himself to "formation" by Christ under the impact of the concrete realities which confront him. This means that Christian decisions are never made in a spaceless and timeless vacuum but in the midst of history, in the midst of a concrete nexus of limiting conditions and conflicting responsibilities which affect the shape of God's will at any particular moment.

The civil rights struggle in America has provided a laboratory experience in which many Christians have had confirmed for them the validity of Bonhoeffer's contextualist approach to Christian decision. Their involvements in the freedom movement were not preceded by a clear-cut program of what Christian faithfulness required of them. They were thrust into the maelstrom of fast-moving, ambiguous events under the conviction that God was present in this movement and that through it the "form of Christ" was taking shape in the lives and actions of men. Only in the immediate context of day-to-day decisions and actions did the will of God become clear to them in a concrete way. Robert W. Spike has made a similar observation in his recent study of the church's participation in the freedom movement:

> It was not until the shadow of turmoil actually touched some white people in the early 1960's, only when they began to break out of the frozen mold of "the way to behave"—in demonstrations and political actions—and were jailed, that the theology became clear. There must be a deed before there can be a doctrine that makes sense. Commitment is not a decision to do something about belief, it is the belief that comes from having acted obediently to Christ, with self-concern pushed to one side.[45]

That is entirely in the spirit of Bonhoeffer. For him, responsible Christian discipleship involves the risk of ever renewed decision under the chastening and instruction of concrete events in which Christ is encountered afresh as the Lord of life. This does not mean that the discernment of the will of God is left to the naïve intuitions of the heart anymore than it may be expected to emerge from a slavish adherence to rules and regulations. "The will of God is not a system of rules which is established from the outset; it is something new and different in each different situation in life, and for this reason a man must ever anew examine what the will of God may be. The heart, the understanding, observation and experience must all collaborate in this task." [46]

[45] *The Freedom Revolution and the Churches* (New York: Association Press, 1965), p. 83.

[46] *Ethics,* p. 161.

Bonhoeffer describes "the structure of responsible life" in terms of a free response to the claims of God and the neighbor. This structure is violated at every point when the Christian conceives of his obligation in terms of a legalistic application of ready-made rules and principles, such as, for example, following the precepts of the Sermon on the Mount as "laws of Christian behavior." Back in 1928 Bonhoeffer saw clearly that this reliance on general norms and principles sacrified the proper Christian relationship to God at the same time as it destroyed man's freedom. To base Christian decision on universally valid moral laws would provide a "way from man to God" and make our relationship with him something which we could control, "a moral action without immediate relationship to God." "Rather must a direct relationship to God's will be ever sought afresh. I do not do something again today because it seemed to me to be good yesterday, but because the will of God points out this way to me today." [47]

Acting according to principle inevitably becomes a subtle kind of self-justification. Through our confident knowledge of good and evil which we have in our possession in the form of ethical principles, we are able to pass judgment on our own acts as well as those of others. Thus we justify our actions by our principles instead of trustfully leaving to God the judgment as to their goodness. The Pharisee is the epitome of the principled man who, with the aid of his principles, attempts to justify himself in his knowledge of good and evil before God, before men, and before himself. In contrast, for the Christian, his deed "is delivered up to God at the moment of its performance."

[47] *No Rusty Swords,* p. 43.

"Ultimate ignorance of one's own good and evil," Bonhoeffer concludes, "and with it a complete reliance upon grace, is an essential property of responsible historical action." [48]

In the second place, Bonhoeffer saw that dependence on principles and laws imperils freedom. "Acting in accordance with principles is unproductive, imitating the law, copying. Acting from freedom is creative." "The Christian stands free, without any protection, before God and before the world, and he alone is wholly responsible for what he does with the gift of freedom." [49] When he wrote the *Ethics,* he appeared to have come to a more positive valuation of the role of principles in ethical decision. Here he sees them as one among many penultimate factors which "prepare the way" for the final decision. "The responsible man acts in the freedom of his own self, without the support of men, circumstances or principles, but with a due consideration for the given human and general conditions *and for the relevant questions of principle. . . .* It is he himself who must observe, judge, weigh up, decide and act." [50] Thus, in the final analysis, it is up to the individual Christian, humbly surrendering to the leading of God, to determine whether and how particular principles should be applied in a concrete situation.

Thirdly, preoccupation with principles as the spring of Christian action undermines the structure of responsible life by cutting the bond with the neighbor and allowing only a partial response to the neighbor's needs. For Bonhoeffer, responsible Christian life is a life of deputyship.

[48] *Ethics,* p. 204.
[49] *No Rusty Swords,* p. 44.
[50] *Ethics,* p. 217; italics mine.

This judgment is again an implication of his Christology. Jesus' life in its very essence was a life of deputyship—a life lived in utter selflessness on behalf of others. "All His living, His action and His dying was deputyship."[51] Deputyship is the form of responsible existence which God wills for all men. In Christ we learn that to be men, that is, men as God intended us to be, is to give ourselves as deputies to our fellowmen, even as Christ revealed himself solely as "the man for others."

As Bonhoeffer sees it, an ethic based on principles proves itself to be inadequate to support such a life of responsible deputyship for others. He makes his point by referring to Immanuel Kant's insistence that the principle of truthfulness requires a man to reveal, when asked, the whereabouts of a friend being pursued by a murderer. Bonhoeffer's commentary is revealing:

> Responsibility is the total and realistic response of man to the claim of God and of our neighbor; but this example shows in its true light how the response of a conscience which is bound by principles is only a partial one. If I refuse to incur guilt against the principle of truthfulness for the sake of my friend, if . . . I refuse to bear guilt for charity's sake, then my action is in contradiction to my responsibility which has its foundation in reality.[52]

Responsible Christian decision and action will always be in correspondence with reality. The Christian who is concerned to meet the neighbor's needs in the concrete situation in which he finds him will not try fanatically to

[51] *Ibid.*, p. 195.
[52] *Ibid.*, p. 214.

impose an absolute principle upon the situation regardless of the resistance offered by the unyielding stuff of reality. Rather, he will try to see "in the given situation what is necessary and what is 'right' for him to grasp and do." [53] This will involve a realistic awareness of the limits which reality imposes upon his action, and the willingness to accept the guilt which comes from having to settle for something less than the perfect realization of an "absolute good."

> Since we are not concerned with the realization of an unretricted principle, it is necessary in the given situation to observe, to weigh up, to assess and to decide always within the limitations of human knowledge in general. . . . One's task is not to turn the world upside-down, but to do what is necessary at the given place and with a due consideration of reality.[54]

The Servant Church in a Secular Age

Bonhoeffer's "due consideration of reality" prompted him, in the closing years of his life, to engage in a sober diagnosis of the cultural and religious situation with which the church of the twentieth century must come to terms in order to maintain its relevance and integrity. Faithfulness to Christ demands the abandonment of all wishful thinking about the situation which the church faces in the modern world. "It is only when we look at reality with open eyes and without any illusions about our morality or our culture that we can believe. Otherwise our faith becomes an illu-

[53] *Ibid.*, p. 197.
[54] *Ibid.*, p. 203.

sion." [55] Neither can the church's witness to the world of our day be kept relevant on the level of verbal communication alone. "The time when men could be told everything by means of words, whether theological or simply pious, is over." [56] Bonhoeffer's last days in prison, therefore, were devoted to reflection on a new form for the church's life and ministry consonant with the new reality of a thoroughly secular age.

The dominant fact about the historical period in which we live which the church must learn to take seriously is its radical secularization. The secularizing process has been going on for a long time, but in our day it has reached its culmination in "a world come of age." "We are proceeding," Bonhoeffer writes, "towards a time of no religion at all: men as they are now simply cannot be religious any more." [57] In all areas of life—science, art, politics, ethics, even religion and philosophy—man's bid for autonomy has been successful, as he has progressively discovered the laws by means of which the world can be understood and controlled. "Man has learned to cope with all questions of importance without recourse to God as a working hypothesis." [58] "God is being increasingly edged out of the world, now that it has come of age." [59]

Bonhoeffer refuses to join in the customary ecclesiastical hand-wringing over this situation. In fact, he welcomes a secular age as an unprecedented opportunity for the gospel. He objects to the kind of apologetic which tries to show

[55] Quoted in Gerhard Ebeling's *Word and Faith* (Philadelphia: Fortress Press, 1963), p. 285.

[56] *Prisoner for God,* p. 122.

[57] *Ibid.*

[58] *Ibid.,* p. 145.

[59] *Ibid.,* p. 156.

that man is at the end of his tether and then brings in a set of "Christian answers" to bail him out of his helplessness and despair. His reasons are threefold:

The attack by Christian apologetic upon the adulthood of the world I consider to be in the first place pointless, in the second ignoble, and in the third un-Christian. Pointless, because it looks to me like an attempt to put a grown-up man back into adolescence, i.e. to make him dependent on things on which he is not in fact dependent any more, thrusting him back into the midst of problems which are in fact not problems for him any more. Ignoble, because this amounts to an effort to exploit the weakness of man for purposes alien to him and not freely subscribed to by him. Un-Christian, because for Christ himself is being substituted one particular stage in the religiousness of man, i.e. a human law.[60]

To "reclaim for Christ a world come of age," we will have to be prepared to dissociate Christianity from religion and work out "a nonreligious interpretation of biblical concepts." [61] This is Bonhoeffer's alternative to Bultmann's demythologizing enterprise, which he criticized mainly because it did not go far enough. The dereligionizing of Christianity which Bonhoeffer proposes is, like his other main themes, an implication of his Christology. It is demanded by the fact that "Christ is no longer an object of religion, but something quite different, indeed and in truth the Lord of the world." [62]

[60] *Ibid.*, p. 147.

[61] Bonhoeffer's own attempt to fill this need in the prison letters is very sketchy. One of the most ambitious attempts to produce such a nonreligious interpretation in a systematic way is Paul M. Van Buren's *The Secular Meaning of the Gospel* (New York: The Macmillan Company, 1963).

[62] *Prisoner for God*, p. 123.

Bonhoeffer's critique of religion as the enemy of faith is similar to Barth's, though it is advanced from a somewhat different perspective dictated by his concern for a worldly Christianity. Bethge summarizes four characteristic features of religion which constitute the basis of Bonhoeffer's rejection of it.[63] First, religion is individualistic. The religious man is so preoccupied with his own inner spiritual states and the cultivation of his own piety that he abandons the world and forgets the needs of the neighbor.

Second, religion is metaphysical. It looks to another world, a supernatural one, to complete this world. Its conception of salvation is not only individualistic but otherworldly. For Bonhoeffer this is a distortion of biblical faith: "It is not with the next world that we are concerned, but with this world as created and preserved and set subject to laws and atoned for and made new. What is above the world is, in the Gospel, intended to exist *for* this world." [64]

Third, religion is provincial. It carves out of the whole of life an enclave which it reserves for itself which is peculiarly religious. With advancing knowledge and secularization, this segment becomes smaller and smaller and is pushed to the periphery of life. Such a restriction of religion to only one department of life inevitably results in its trivialization. By contrast, "Christ takes hold of a man in the centre of his life." [65] "God is the 'beyond' in the midst of our life. The Church stands not where human powers give out, on the borders, but in the centre of the village." [66]

[63] "Challenge of Bonhoeffer's Life and Theology," pp. 33-34.
[64] *Prisoner for God,* p. 126.
[65] *Ibid.,* p. 154.
[66] *Ibid.,* p. 124.

Fourth, religion appeals to a God who operates as a *Deus ex machina,* who is always intervening to provide the answers to life's problems and the solutions to its distresses and conflicts. The God of religion is a kind of cosmic bellhop whose services run the gamut from theoretical explanations for as yet unsolved scientific and metaphysical questions (a "god of the gaps") to practical answers to personal and social needs. Bonhoeffer summarizes the decisive difference between this sort of God and the suffering God of the Bible in these words:

> Man's religiosity makes him look in his distress to the power of God in the world; he uses God as a *Deus ex machina.* The Bible however directs him to the powerlessness and suffering of God; only a suffering God can help. To this extent we may say that the process we have described by which the world came of age was an abandonment of a false conception of God, and a clearing of the decks for the God of the Bible, who conquers power and space in the world by his weakness.[67]

How much these strictures touch religion in its entirety, or just religion in its perverted, idolatrous forms, is a moot question. Daniel Jenkins has criticized Bonhoeffer, no doubt with good reason, for "working with an unduly negative interpretation of religion," [68] which fails to recognize the way in which faith as well as sin continues to generate religion even in a world come of age. Be that as it may, Bonhoeffer has undoubtedly scored decisively at a number of points where the contemporary church is highly vulnerable. Its individualistic piety, its otherworldly

[67] *Ibid.,* p. 164.
[68] *Beyond Religion* (Philadelphia: Westminster Press, 1962), p. 34.

escapism, its clubby provincialism, its utilitaran religiosity have all too often incapacitated it from being a faithful and effective servant of God and man in our secular age.

This does not mean that Bonhoeffer was ready to give up on the church as some of his would-be followers have been inclined to do. Bethge, who was as close to Bonhoeffer as anyone, warns that "it would be a great mistake to understand Bonhoeffer as abolishing the worshiping church and replacing service and sacrament by charity acts." [69] It is clear, however, that he called for a drastic revamping of the church's stance in the contemporary world, not simply in order to be responsive to the challenge of a secular age but in order to allow the church to *be* the church, in order to fulfill its essential nature and mission as the body of Christ.

The church in a secular age, as in any age, must be a servant church. If she is truly that fellowship of men in which Christ is being formed, the only form appropriate to her nature is the servant form. If Jesus is the man for others, then "the Church is her true self only when she exists for humanity." "She must take her part in the social life of the world," Bonhoeffer goes on to say, "not lording it over men, but helping and serving them. She must tell men, whatever their calling, what it means to live in Christ, to exist for others." [70] In the secular milieu of our modern world, in which men have increasing difficulty in grasping the meaning of divine transcendence, the church can embody that meaning only by showing the world the picture of "man existing for others, and hence the Crucified." [71]

[69] "Challenge of Bonhoeffer's Life and Theology," p. 35.
[70] *Prisoner for God*, p. 180.
[71] *Ibid.*, p. 179.

This selfless existence on behalf of others, maintained to the point of death, may be the only convincing bearer of transcendence which the secular man of today can make any sense of.

There is deep pathos in Bonhoeffer's discussion of the contemporary church's apostasy from its servant role and his hints about the mode of its renewal. "During these years the Church has fought for self-preservation as though it were a end in itself, and has thereby lost its chance to speak a word of reconciliation to mankind and the world at large." [72] This means that, for the time being at least, "the Christian cause will be a silent and hidden affair, but there will be those who pray and do right and wait for God's own time." [73] While it is waiting for the ripening of God's good purposes, the church will maintain its "secret discipline," carefully preserving the mysteries of the faith from profanization by the world. It will give itself unostentatiously to the ministry of human need without seeking credit or prestige for extending the cup of cold water or the helping hand. It will thrust itself fully into the life of the world and "drink the earthly cup to the lees," sharing there in the sufferings of its crucified and risen Lord. In this direction alone lies the road to renewal. Only thus will it stand a chance to *be* the church once again. Only as a servant church, pursuing its worldly mission in selfless and silent suffering, can it earn the right to speak with authority and power to our secular age.

In the midst of his earlier struggles to renew the German church in the face of overwhelming temptations to apostasy, Bonhoeffer once remarked: "Only those who cry

[72] *Ibid.*, p. 140.
[73] *Ibid.*, p. 141.

for the Jews are allowed to sing Gregorian chants." [74] A contemporary translation of that dictum for the church in America might well run as follows: Only those who cry for the Negroes in their drive for freedom and justice; only those who weep for the poor in the urban tenements and rural shacks of our land; only those who share in the sufferings of the victims of war and social strife, and the more incalculable hurts of the lonely, the despised, and forsaken of our society; only these have the right to raise their voices in praise to God in the hymns and prayers of the church. For they alone represent the church in its true essence as the suffering servant-people of God.

[74] Quoted in "Challenge of Bonhoeffer's Life and Theology," p. 35.

VII

THEOLOGICAL RESOURCES FOR THE RENEWAL OF THE CHURCH

A widely pervasive concern for the renewal of the church in our time has been a striking feature of much recent Christian writing and discussion. This concern has come to the surface in such a wide variety of manifestations that Bishop John A. T. Robinson is constrained to raise the question in the title of a recent book whether a "new reformation" is not in fact in the process of being born. The ferment goes on at many levels. It is seen in the forces of renewal unleashed in Roman Catholicism by Pope John's call for an *aggiornamento* or updating of the forms of the church's faith and life. It is evident in the selection of "renewal" as the theme for the Fourth Assembly of the World Council of Churches scheduled for 1968. It has produced an *Honest to God* in England and *The Comfortable Pew* in Canada, searching and prophetic books which evoked such an astonishing reaction that they stand out as omens of renewal and reform. In the United States the impetus for renewal has come in response to an increasing disenchantment with the failure of the church, despite its phenomenal statistical successes, to break out of the graveclothes of a massively institutionalized culture-religion which has all but lost its prophetic voice. The racial crisis and its probing of the Christian conscience, the revolt of college students against the sterility of institutional religion, the challenge of an increasingly secularized urban culture and its indifference to the church—these and other pressures have forced an agonizing reappraisal of the present forms of the church's life and witness.

The renewal for which many sensitive churchmen are so earnestly looking today should be clearly differentiated from the much less radical phenomenon of the revival. Indeed, it might be said that the perpetuation of eighteenth-century patterns of revivalism in the present-day church constitutes one of the major barriers to genuine renewal.[1] The anti-intellectualism, emotionalism, and individualism characteristic of revivalistic Christainity only serves to accentuate the growing irrelevance of the church in the face of the dynamic forces of secularization and urbanization which shape so decisively the life of contemporary man.

The call for renewal being heard today is for something much more radical than the stimulation of individual piety and spiritual commitment. It is a call for a basic rethinking of the forms in which the Christian gospel can be conveyed with effectiveness and integrity to the contemporary mind, as well as a fundamental restructuring of the church's life to reflect more adequately its true nature and mission. Some are prepared to dismiss this ferment in the church as an abortive tinkering with the

[1] Cf. Gibson Winter's critique of the coalition between denominational Christianity and revivalism as evidenced in the widespread support of the Billy Graham crusades, resulting in an inordinate preoccupation with "pietism" at the expense of "servanthood." *The New Creation as Metropolis* (New York: The Macmillan Company, 1963), pp. 12-20.

ecclesiastical machinery, a passing fad of the avant-garde whose itching ears are always atilt to catch whatever "new winds of doctrine" may be blowing. Others appraise it as evidence of a new sensitivity to what the Spirit may be saying to the churches in an age of revolutionary change. They see it as the first lapping on the beach of what could well become a mighty tide of renewal sweeping away the dead driftwood of sterile and outmoded beliefs and practices and infusing new life and power into the Christian movement in our time.

One indication that the current of renewal beginning to flow in the life of the church may merit this more positive judgment is the fact that it owes much of its inspiration to the prophetic probing of a generation of unusually fertile theological minds. If renewal comes to the church in our time, it will, to be sure, be the result of the revivifying activity of the Spirit of God, making dead bones come to new life as sensitive men and women are inspired to a new obedience to Christ's lordship in thought and life. The fact that renewal is ultimately the work of God does not preclude, however, the necessity of human agents of renewal. It has been the thesis of this book that in the ranks of contemporary theologians one can find some of the most promising agents of renewal in the church today. In the foregoing chapters we have sought to uncover certain salient features in the thought of five of them which seem to have the richest potential for inspiring and directing the movement of church renewal. It remains for us to draw some general conclusions as to the significance of these theological resources for renewal which have emerged from our study.

Diagnoses of the church's ills and prescriptions for its

renewal and reform are by no means in short supply these days. The superficiality and banality of some of them makes one chary about any attempt to draw up a blueprint. If, as it has been said about the civil rights struggle, it is impossible to "schedule a revolution," it is equally futile to try to "program a renewal" in the life of the church. At the same time, renewal is not likely to take place in any significant degree unless certain preconditions are met which reflect God's ways of working in his world and in his church, and which a faithful theological inquiry enables us, at least to some extent, to specify. Our efforts in these pages to listen attentively to what some of contemporary theology's most prophetic voices are saying have issued in at least a few tentative conclusions concerning the shape and style appropriate for a renewed church in the second half of the twentieth century.

1. *Such a renewed church will exhibit a radical responsiveness to the Word of God as the norm by which it consistently judges its life.*

One of the most alarming symptoms of the crisis confronting the church today is its increasing bondage to cultural norms which are antithetical to the Christianity of the New Testament. This spurious secularization of the Christian faith has proceeded, by and large, hand-in-hand with a continuing profession of allegiance to the Bible, with little conscious awareness that biblical faith was in fact imperceptibly being eroded away. Ironically, it has often been the most "Bible-believing" fundamentalists who have accorded the most uncritical obeisance to cultural myths associated with racism, materialism, and nationalistic chauvinism. The invasion of the church by these false secularisms is all the more dangerous because of the subtle and often subliminal nature of the take-over. The true nature of the peril is well expressed by Gayraud S. Wilmore when he says that "if there is a kind of worldliness based upon illusions, if there is a worldliness standing over against the realism of faith, it is this child of the unholy alliance between pietistic Christianity and patronizing Americanism." [2]

In a provocative new book Harvey Cox has depicted one of the central roles of the church as that of "cultural exorcist."[3] The modern equivalent of casting out demons is the emancipation of men from those social myths which keep them in bondage to illusions and compulsive behavior patterns with respect to such matters as race, class, and sex, and thus inhibit their growth into mature manhood. The church is today heir to this same ministry of exorcism which was its Lord's. Unfortunately, like some of the disciples of old (Luke 9:40), it is often impotent to cast out these modern cultural demons because it has allowed itself to become imprisoned by the same myths which govern so pervasively the attitudes and behavior patterns of non-Christian members of our society. The renewal of the church in our day is contingent upon its ability to neutralize the power of these social and cultural forces which disfigure its life, distort its message, and deter its mission.

The power to turn back these subtle encroachments by alien cultural influences can come from only one source—the recovery by the church of a new sensitivity to the living Word of God as mediated through the Bible. Such a radical return to biblical integrity is a *sine qua non* of renewal.

[2] *The Secular Relevance of the Church* (Philadelphia: Westminster Press, 1962), p. 32.

[3] *The Secular City* (New York: The Macmillan Company, 1965), ch. 7.

However much the theology of our day may have moved on from some of Barth's positions, those who are interested in the renewal of the church cannot afford to overlook the prophetic significance of his call to radical openness and obedience to the Word of God.

This is no "back to the Bible" fundamentalist sloganeering. It is a simple recognition that the church in order to *be* the church must take seriously the fountainhead of its faith—the New Testament witness to the Word of God. Barth is capable of being of great help in showing how it is possible to take the Bible with utmost seriousness as the medium of God's contemporary address without at the same time falling into a wooden biblicism and enslaving literalism. He has taught the twentieth-century Protestant churches that they can be free from entangling pressures emanating from the cultural environment, and hence speak with a genuinely prophetic voice only when they stand under the perpetual judgment of the Word of God. Thanks to him, the church has been encouraged to see the Bible as constitutive of its very life, and the principle of standing under the Word of God as the source and power of its continuing renewal.

Where the church has heeded this summons to biblical integrity, where it has returned to the original font of its faith as it did in the sixteenth-century Reformation, it has found fresh currents of renewal and reform stirring within it. Only when it begins to wrestle seriously in concrete terms with its mission to today's world in the light of its charter in the New Testament will it begin to show the distinctive and authentic marks of the servant people of God. Only when it begins to attend earnestly in its preaching and study to what God is saying and doing in the tumultuous events of today's rapidly changing order, in the light of what he said and did in the foundational events which originally brought the church into being, will it speak in accents clearly distinguishable from the siren voices of an alien culture.

2. The emphasis on restoring the proclamation of the Word of God to a place of central importance in the life of the church as the prerequisite of renewal is Barth's most notable legacy. Bultmann, as we have seen, has shared Barth's concern for the centrality of proclamation. While Barth has been concerned to recall theology to faithful conformity to the revelation of God given once and for all in biblical history, Bultmann has stressed (perhaps with too little emphasis on the historical roots of faith) the contemporaneous character of the Word of God as a Word addressed to us in the here and now. The crucial salvation-event is not something restricted to past history, but something that happens again and again when through the preaching of the church God acts to challenge men to the venture of authentic Christian faith and obedience.

The church's preaching, however, will not be productive of such saving and transforming encounters with the Word of God *unless it finds fresh and authentic ways of proclaiming the essential affirmations of biblical faith in language intelligible to contemporary man.* Until the church finds ways of resolving what Bishop Robinson has called its "currency crisis" brought on by the breakdown of traditional means of Christian communication, renewal will elude it. To this crisis many voices in contemporary theology have spoken prophetically. Most notably has this been true in the case of Bultmann's demythologizing and existential reinterpretation of Scripture, Tillich's deliteralizing interpretation of the symbols of faith in the context of an "answering theology," and Bonhoeffer's search for a nonreligious interpretation of biblical concepts.

A New Testament scholar, Eduard Schweizer, has made the observation that one of the characteristic signs of the Spirit of God is that he always speaks in modern language, addressing men in terms of their contemporary situation. "If this were not the case," he writes,

> it would be best to put the sermons of Paul and Peter on a tape recording and to play them in our services, instead of training ministers who are, in spite of their expensive training, not always on the level of Peter and Paul. A sermon without burning love towards modern man, a sermon in an outlived language, no longer understandable in a modern world, is probably no sermon of the Holy Spirit.[4]

One of the factors inhibiting renewal today is the relic of an "outlived language" which encumbers so much of the church's speech. When the revolutionary dynamism of the gospel fails to find vehicles of truly contemporary expression, an honest and vital response to its claims and promises is rendered impossible. At this point, Tillich's attempt to show how the affirmations of Christian faith answer to fundamental questions which modern men are really asking is a forceful reminder of the need for contemporary relevance in the church's preaching and teaching. So also is Bultmann's effort to expose the true scandal of the gospel by penetrating through the mythical expressions of the New Testament and enabling them to come

[4] The Relation of Scripture, Church Tradition and Modern Interpretation" in *New Theology No. 1* ed. by Martin E. Marty and Dean G. Peerman (New York: The Macmillan Company, 1964), p. 49.

alive in terms of their concrete and existential meaning for us today.

There is doubtless room for a variety of approaches to the problem of contemporizing the church's language. But if the Holy Spirit is to be free to work within the church, he must find a living language through which to speak. This requires that the church learn to "sit loose" to particular verbal forms through which its faith has long been expressed. "Where the Spirit of the Lord is, there is liberty." Genuine renewal will come only when the church is liberated from a reactionary literalism which imprisons the living Word in the opaque words of a dead language. Ways must be found, for example, to deliteralize biblical myth and symbol so as to remove the necessity of an arbitrary sacrifice of the intellect on the part of those who would take it seriously.

In order for this to take place, the church must provide a hospitable home for honest doubt, welcoming it as a mark of the seriousness of faith. The suppression of doubt, as Tillich has reminded us, drives faith into either profane or demonic distortions. Either it becomes a superficial and trivial embellishment of life, lacking the depth of an ultimate concern, or it becomes pathologically defensive, committed dogmatically to particular intellectual formulations of the faith which are removed from all possibility of doubt or question. If renewal is to come in the church, this freezing of the faith into inflexible verbal formulas must give way to a genuine openness to the possibility that the Spirit can speak in a variety of tongues. Resources abound in the work of the church's theologians to assist it in proclaiming the ancient gospel in "tongues" which are intelligible to twentieth-century men and women. The sheer sense of liberation which greets a book like *Honest to God* attests to the possibilities of renewal which could be realized with a wider dissemination in the church of these modern "translations" of the gospel.

3. The renewal of the church comes through a radical responsiveness to the Word of God. The power of the Word of God to renew and transform the community of God's people, however, is dependent on its proclamation in language which is understandable within our contemporary situation. Its renewing power is further contingent upon *the radical openness of the church to the world as the sphere within which God calls it to contemporary obedience.*

This means that a church which is in the constant process of renewing itself lives in an inevitable twofold tension. We have had ample occasion to point out the tension between biblical integrity and contemporary relevance. We must be true to the past history which defines who we are as the people of God, as well as the present time in which God confronts us anew and lays his claim upon us. We must also learn to live in another tension—the tension between the church and the world. More than any other theologian Bonhoeffer has taught us that it is only within this tension, as the church enters into responsible and costly engagement with worldly structures, that the Word of God comes to concrete expression. From him we have learned again what was already clear in the New Testament, that the church exists for the sake of humanity and not for its own sake.

In response to this kind of prophetic voice from the church's theologians in recent years, the World Council of Churches set in motion in 1961 a long-range study on

"The Missionary Structure of the Congregation." Out of this study has been developing a viewpoint which, to quote Colin Williams,

> insists that the present structures of the church are so dominated by the church's surrender to its own worldly security, and that the church is so imprisoned within the expensive facades of buildings that relate to men only in a very limited portion of their life, that she can find renewal only as she surrenders these securities and pours herself out upon the world, careless of her own safety or reputation or wealth, allowing the *forms* of her renewed life to grow around *all the shapes of worldly need.*[5]

In a very real sense, this means that the church which would share in the servant ministry of its Lord must be prepared to "let the world write the agenda." [6]

If the church is to move out into the world in the performance of its servant task, it must be armed with a sober Christian realism which fortifies it to serve effectively and responsibly in the midst of controversy and compromise. At this point, the thought of Reinhold Niebuhr becomes immensely fruitful by showing how Christian love can become relevant to the needs of men in society only when it employs the necessary instruments of justice, including the use of power. True servanthood in the world is impossible without suffering, tension, and participation in power conflicts. The church which is unwilling to face the implications of such involvement in the world has abdicated its servant role in the interests of its own inner peace

[5] *Where in the World?* (New York: National Council of Churches, 1963), p. 59. Used by permission of Colin Williams.

[6] *Ibid.*, p. 75.

and harmony. In a memorable passage Gibson Winter has described the apostasy of much of the church today in this regard, and the price it must pay for its renewal:

Men and women today look to the local congregation as a haven from conflict and tension. Clergymen view their work as the maintenance of harmonious relationships within the flock; the frictionless machine is the ideal image of the congregation. The creation of such *harmonious enclaves* is an indication of the utter dislocation of the Church in our society. The Church is intended to be a *suffering body* in the world, showing forth the Lord's death until He come. This community in Christ is not called to sacrifice its ministry of reconciliation in order to preserve its inner tranquility. This body is called to bear within itself the sufferings imposed upon it by a ministry of reconciliation within the broken communication of the world. Reopening broken communication will inevitably tear and disrupt the internal life of the Church, but that inner suffering is the essential nature of the authentic presence of the New Mankind in the world.[7]

The World Council study mentioned above has raised the question as to whether it may be appropriate to speak of "heretical structures" of the congregation in much the same way as we speak of "heretical doctrines." A heretical structure would be one which distorts the way in which God relates to the world through the church and hence frustrates his mission in the world. "If Church structures train believers only to practice the presence of Christ within the Christian community; and therefore fail to train them to recognize Christ's presence at the points of

[7] *New Creation as Metropolis*, p. 127.

worldly need and to serve Christ at *that* altar; then those structures are heretical." [8] One of the most persistent concerns among those seeking the renewal of the church has been to find new forms of church life to replace such heretical structures—forms which give contemporary shape and substance to the New Testament understanding of the church as the suffering servant people of God.

4. Two main obstacles to renewal have emerged during the course of our discussion: the absolutizing of traditional verbalizations of faith which fail to communicate the true scandal of the Christian message to our contemporaries; and the inertia of institutional forms which impede the church's mission to the world. Both these tendencies in the church represent a kind of fundamentalism (in the first case, doctrinal, in the second, structural or morphological fundamentalism) [9] which resists all change in the belief that God has invested his revelation in static forms which are immune to historical development. This deification of the forms of a bygone day is one of the most dangerous kinds of idolatry against which the church must fight for its life. The freezing of both doctrine and organization by an incipient fundamentalism is the real enemy in the way of renewal today. A renewed church will decisively reject this fundamentalist heresy as it demonstrates its *freedom from the idolatry of verbal and institutional forms.*

Tillich's Protestant principle points in the direction of the theological resource by means of which this all-important condition for renewal is to be realized. The church

[8] *Where in the World?* p. 83.

[9] This term "morphological fundamentalism" has come into wide usage in recent discussions of renewal. Cf. *Ibid.,* pp. 11-12.

which takes seriously the Protestant principle will refrain from investing the "earthen vessels" of its historically conditioned doctrinal formulations and church structures with any final sanctity. It will claim no ultimate holiness for any of its words or organizational forms. It will leave to God the justification of its language and the shape of its life. Thus it will have built into it the principle of its own reformation and the freedom for self-criticism so essential to its renewal. This freedom is the gift of a God who graciously comes to us through human words and institutions, but who refuses to be bound by them or clothe them with the holiness which belongs only to him.

When temporal forms of speech or organization are made into idols by removing them from historical criticism and elevating them to eternal significance, the streams of renewal are effectively quenched in the life of the church. At such times there is the need for Christian iconoclasts who will break the images and shatter the idols which men falsely worship. Some of the church's most prophetic theologians are today performing this essential iconoclastic task—plowing up the arid ground of the church's life and thought in preparation for an eventual harvest, breaking down in order ultimately to build up. If the church is mature enough to listen to these voices of its theological prophets, it will succeed in being the *ecclesia semper reformanda,* the church which is always in the process of being reformed.

SUGGESTIONS FOR FURTHER READING

These biographical suggestions are far from a complete listing of either primary or secondary sources for the theologians included in our study. They are intended as a guide for the uninitiated reader who is in need of counsel as to where most profitably to begin his study of a particular theologian, as well as some clues as to what books are most helpful in giving a more comprehensive and balanced understanding of the man's thought. For the most part, works of a highly technical nature have been omitted.

I. Karl Barth

The best way into the mature Barth is probably through *The Humanity of God* (John Knox Press, 1960), a book of three essays which includes Barth's often witty reflections on his own theological pilgrimage. Another good beginning point is *Evangelical Theology: An Introduction* (Holt, Reinhart and Winston, 1963), which contains the lectures delivered on his 1962 American tour. Before tackling the long shelf of the *Church Dogmatics,* which is now published in English in twelve volumes (T. and T. Clark, 1936-60), the reader may want to sample *Church Dogmatics: A Selection* by Helmut Gollwitzer (Torchbooks ed., Harper, 1962) . A reliable guide through the complex maze of the *Dogmatics* is provided by Arnold B. Come in his *An Introduction to Barth's "Dogmatics" for Preachers* (Westminster Press, 1963), which includes an excellent chapter on "How to Avoid Becoming a Barthian."

Earlier epochal works include *The Epistle to the Romans* (Oxford University Press, 1933), the exegetical work which launched the Barthian revolution in modern theology; *The Word of God and the Word of Man* (Torchbooks ed., 1957), containing a number of early essays and addresses; and *Natural Theology* (Geoffrey Bles, 1946), Barth's spirited debate with Brunner. Georges Casalis has written a revealing *Portrait of Karl Barth* (Doubleday, 1963), with a fine introduction by Robert McAfee Brown. Two important systematic expositions of Barth's thought are to be found in G. C. Berkouwer's *The Triumph of Grace in the Theology of Karl Barth* (Eerdmans, 1956) and Herbert Hartwell's *The Theology of Karl Barth* (Westminster,1964).

II. Rudolf Bultmann

The best place to begin a study of Bultmann is his programmatic essay "New Testament and Mythology," which precipitated the demythologizing debate in *Kerygma and Myth,* edited by H. W. Bartsch (Torchbooks ed., 1961). Perhaps the most readable exposition of his basic viewpoint is his *Jesus Christ and Mythology* (Macmillan, 1962). Among his major works are: *Essays Philosophical and Theological* (SCM Press, 1955); *History and Eschatology: The Presence of Eternity* (Torchbooks ed., 1962), his

1955 Gifford Lectures; and his monumental two-volume work, *The Theology of the New Testament* (Scribner's, 1955).

The volume of secondary works on Bultmann and the issues which he has raised is enormous. Among the most helpful are the following: Carl E. Braaten and Roy A. Harrisville (eds.), *Kerygma and History* (Abingdon Press, 1962), a symposium of critical essays on Bultmann's theology by Lutheran theologians; David Cairns, *A Gospel Without Myth? Bultmann's Challenge to the Preacher* (SCM Press, 1960), which includes an analysis of some of Bultmann's sermons which show, Cairns believes, that he does not practice in the pulpit what he preaches in his study; Ian Henderson, *Myth in the New Testament* (SCM, 1952), the first brief, critical study of Bultmann to appear in English; two books by John Macquarrie, *An Existentialist Theology* (SCM, 1955), a careful study of Bultmann's use of key concepts of Heidegger, and *The Scope of Demythologizing* (Harper, 1960), the best available study of the debate between Bultmann and his critics, balanced, sympathetic, and eminently readable; Giovanni Miegge, *Gospel and Myth* (John Knox Press, 1960), a perceptive analysis by a Waldensian scholar; and Schubert Ogden, *Christ Without Myth* (Harper, 1961), the attempt of a young American theologian to pursue Bultmann's demythologizing program further than does Bultmann himself.

III. Paul Tillich

For the beginner, Tillich's books of sermons constitute the best introduction: *The Shaking of the Foundations*

(Scribner's, 1948); *The New Being* (Scribner's, 1955); *The Eternal Now* (Scribner's, 1963). Tillich's fully developed system of philosophical theology is found in his *Systematic Theology,* published in three volumes by the University of Chicago Press, 1951, 1957, and 1963. Among his most significant shorter works are the following: *Dynamics of Faith* (Torchbooks ed., 1958); *The Courage to Be* (Yale University Press, 1952); *Love, Power, and Justice* (Galaxy ed., 1954); *Morality and Beyond* (Harper, 1963); and *Theology of Culture* (Oxford University Press, 1959), a collection of important occasional essays.

The Theology of Paul Tillich, edited by Charles W. Kegley and Robert W. Bretall (Macmillan, 1952), is a collection of critical studies of Tillich's thought by leading theologians together with Tillich's own reply to his critics. An appreciative but critical study of Tillich's Christology has been made by a Roman Catholic theologian: George H. Tavard, *Paul Tillich and the Christian Message* (Scribner's, 1962). One of the best systematic expositions of Tillich's theology along with a Barthian style criticism is Alexander J. McKelway's *The Systematic Theology of Paul Tillich* (John Knox Press, 1964). Finally, a good book for clarifying many issues in Tillich's thought, a transcript of actual dialogues with students, is *Ultimate Concern: Tillich in Dialogue,* edited by D. Mackenzie Brown (Harper, 1965).

IV. Reinhold Niebuhr

Perhaps the best initial exposure to Niebuhr is obtained by reading some of his occasional essays and articles in which theological and social analyses are blended to illuminate contemporary problems. These may be found in two volumes of selected writings edited by D. B. Robertson: *Love and Justice* (Westminster, 1957), and *Essays in Applied Christianity* (Meridian Books, 1959). The journal *Christianity and Crisis* continues to carry, as it has for many years, Niebuhr's searching commentary on the contemporary scene. The serious reader of Niebuhr will waste no time in getting to his *magnum opus,* the Gifford Lectures on *The Nature and Destiny of Man* (Scribner's, 1949). Pivotal works which show Niebuhr's developing thought are *Leaves from the Notebooks of a Tamed Cynic* (Meridian Books, 1957), revealing autobiographical reflections on his experiences in the pastorate; *Moral Man and Immoral Society* (Scribner's, 1932), a realistic analysis of the difference between individual and group morality; *An Interpretation of Christian Ethics* (Harper, 1935); *The Children of Light and the Children of Darkness* (Scribner's, 1944), a study of democracy from the standpoint of Christian realism; *Faith and History: A Comparison of Christian and Modern Views of History* (Scribner's, 1949); *Christian Realism and Political Problems* (Scribner's, 1953); *The Self and the Dramas of History* (Scribner's, 1955).

Among the secondary literature on Niebuhr, by far the best work is Gordan Harland's *The Thought of Reinhold Niebuhr* (Oxford University Press, 1960). *Reinhold Niebuhr: His Religious, Social, and Political Thought* (Macmillan, 1956) contains a group of interpretive essays by leading theologians and Niebuhr's reply. June Bingham has written an intimate biographical and interpretive study: *Courage to Change: An Introduction to the life and Thought of Reinhold Niebuhr* (Scribner's, 1961).

V. Dietrich Bonhoeffer

Most people make their first acquaintance with Bonhoeffer through his *Letters and Papers from Prison,* edited by Eberhard Bethge (SCM, 1953). The American edition is entitled *Prisoner for God* (Macmillan, 1954). Two other nontechnical works from Bonhoeffer's middle period are still widely read today: *The Cost of Discipleship* (Macmillan, 1948), which includes an exposition of the Sermon on the Mount; and *Life Together* (Harper, 1954). A more difficult work, *Ethics,* also edited by Eberhard Bethge (Macmillian, 1955), is essential to an understanding of Bonhoeffer's more mature theology. The earlier roots of his theology can be studied in two scholarly works: *The Communion of Saints* (Harper, 1963), a study of the doctrine of the church, and *Act and Being* (Harper, 1962).

Considerable helpful interpretive literature has been appearing in the last few years, including two books by John D. Godsey: *The Theology of Dietrich Bonhoeffer* (Westminster, 1960), a running exposition of Bonhoeffer's major works, and a short popular introduction with two of Bonhoeffer's shorter writings, *Preface to Bonhoeffer* (Fortress Press, 1965). A helpful source for getting Bonhoeffer's developing thought in perspective is "The Challenge of Dietrich Bonhoeffer's Life and Theology" in *The Chicago Theological Seminary Register,* February, 1961, by Bonhoeffer's close friend Eberhard Bethge. A book of critical essays on various aspects of Bonhoeffer's theology has been edited by Martin E. Marty entitled *The Place of Bonhoeffer* (Association Press, 1962).

INDEX

SHENANDOAH UNIVERSITY LIBRARY
WINCHESTER, VA 22601